Estate Planning Made Simple

Merle E. Dowd

Edited and prepared for publication by The Stonesong Press, Inc.

A MADE SIMPLE BOOK

DOUBLEDAY

NEW YORK   LONDON   TORONTO   SYDNEY   AUCKLAND

Edited and prepared for publication by The Stonesong Press, Inc.
Managing Editor: Sheree Bykofsky
Editor: Sarah Gold
Production Assistant: Kathryn A. Clark
Design: Blackbirch Graphics, Inc.

A MADE SIMPLE BOOK

Published by Doubleday, a division of
Bantam Doubleday Dell Publishing Group, Inc.
666 Fifth Avenue, New York, New York 10103

MADE SIMPLE and DOUBLEDAY are trademarks of Doubleday,
a division of Bantam Doubleday Dell Publishing Group, Inc.

Library of Congress Cataloging-in-Publication Data
Dowd, Merle E.
    Estate planning made simple/ Merle E. Dowd; edited and prepared for
publication by the Stonesong Press, Inc. — 1st ed.
    p.   cm.
    A MADE SIMPLE BOOK.
    1. Estate planning—United States—Popular works   I. Stonesong
Press. II. Title.
KF750.Z9D685 1991
346.7305'2—dc20   90-25010
ISBN 0-385-41638-5   CIP

9 8 7 6 5 4 3

CONTENTS

The First Step

Planning your estate simply means preparing for the orderly transition and distribution of your assets following your death. The key word is orderly.

Your first step in preparing for the inevitable is to make up your mind to take action. Leaving an orderly trail for others to follow is critical if the transition is to be orderly. Organizing your affairs, leaving a written record of your wishes, and appointing a person to supervise the conveyance of your property is really all there is to most estate plans. Yet, only about 3 out of 10 people leave a valid will or a living trust to guide family and heirs.

If you don't prepare a will or living trust, the state where you live has one already written for you. Buried in your state's code is a "law of succession," a one-size-fits-all plan drawn by your state's legislature to govern the distribution of a person's assets if no countervailing legal document assumes precedence. That chilling fact alone should motivate you to direct a personal representative, whether an executor or trustee, to wind up your affairs and distribute your assets according to your wishes—not according to some bureaucrat's uniform application of the law.

Estate planning is part of your overall financial planning efforts. Financial planning is sometimes the object of media hype. Just as often financial planners are damned by regulators and clients for less than professional conduct. But if a financial planner can attract your attention and motivate you to develop an estate plan, then he or she has done you a service. A better plan is to use this book as a guide to help you plan your estate yourself.

Financial planning encompasses five activities: Saving, insurance, investment, achieving life goals that require funding, and estate planning. Investing is the fun part. The possibility of making your money grow—of jousting or matching wits with the best brains on Wall Street—can be exciting. The dream of making money with money attracts millions of investors to the market. Capital acquisition (saving) and estate planning comprise the drearier activities. But they can also be the most important.

Why do so few persons write even simple wills or develop living trusts? Surveys have unearthed a few reasons. The most common ones fall into the following categories:

Superstition

Some persons actually believe that drafting a will or planning their estate might accelerate their death. Just thinking about it could make it happen, they think. If superstition is keeping you from thinking about what will happen to your property or preparing your spouse to manage your estate, you need to face up to the reality of your situation. If you don't act, the state will. It's that simple.

Prospect of Death

Most people recognize the inevitability of their own death, but thinking about it can be morbid or depressing for some. Not wanting to face their mortality causes them to procrastinate. And make no mistake, planning your estate involves thinking about and accepting your death. The two go together. Not thinking about an estate plan accomplishes no useful purpose.

Not Needed Now

"It's too soon to even think about an estate plan," is another excuse. How soon is too soon? If you could plan how long you were going to live, waiting until a few weeks or months before that final event would be okay. But none of us is privy to that information. Statistics may be in your favor, as life expectancies continue to lengthen. But statistics also indicate that many persons are killed in accidents or die from early onset of heart failure and other diseases. Most of us can't be absolutely certain that we will be around tomorrow. Given this situation, today is none too soon to begin to plan your estate. If you are young and healthy, you may revise your estate plan a dozen times before death. Better that than dying intestate—without a will.

The following chapters outline what you need to know to put your own estate plan together. Knowing the size of your estate is critical, because it affects taxes and what you may want to do about gifts and charitable contributions. Completing the numerous worksheets in Chapter 2 will help you assemble the facts and data you need to get started. Chapter 3 explains federal and state estate and inheritance taxes. Chapters

4 and 5 will help you to prepare a will or a living trust and decide which might be better suited to your situation. Trusts other than the living trust (Chapter 6) are devices for gaining income while leaving portions of your estate to charities. Joint ownership (Chapter 7) can be controversial and is often misunderstood. Chapter 8 explains how gifts can be a powerful tool in estate planning to avoid or minimize taxes. Insurance (Chapter 9) may be necessary to provide the cash needed for paying estate taxes. Chapter 10 is vitally important for those persons who live in the nine community property states, as law, regulations, and taxes are different in those states from the other 41 and the District of Columbia. Chapter 11 sets up a plan for managing your estate and helps you reduce the workload of your executor or trustee. Final instructions, noted in Chapter 12, help survivors cope with the aftermath of your death.

Caution: Seek counsel for the final drafting of your will or living trust. Far too much is riding on the outcome of your planning activities to take a chance on botching the final job. This book will help you formulate your ideas, make decisions, and reduce the time and expense involved in consulting a professional. But do bring in a professional to develop the actual legal documents that will make it all happen according to your plan. You can't afford to take chances because you will not be around to make corrections when your final plan goes into effect.

CHAPTER ONE

Why You Should Plan Your Estate

KEY TERMS FOR THIS CHAPTER

estate planning	*decedent*
conveyance	*intestate*
executor	*probate court*
administrator	*living trust*
personal representative	*appraiser*

If you think that estate planning means drafting a will, you are looking at only a small part of the process. **Estate planning** represents the fifth step in lifelong financial planning, that is, the year-after-year process of getting the most living value from your money. The four steps that precede estate planning involve:

- collecting capital—saving;
- setting up protection limits to manage risk—insurance;
- putting your collected capital to work— investing;
- achieving your major life goals that involve money, such as paying for your children's education, establishing your own business, or planning for retirement.

Estate Planning—What Is It?

Estate planning means planning for the orderly **conveyance** or legal distribution of your property to heirs. That's the big picture. But to complete the picture, the myriad details filling the background must be brought into focus. For example, if a major part of your wealth is wrapped up in boutiques selling women's fashions, you may not want your two sons who are engineers to take over their ownership and management. Instead, you might look at a plan that would permit key employees to take over the business with a long term payout to the estate.

An estate plan calls for an **executor, administrator,** or **personal representative** to manage the conveyance of your property. If your estate plan indicates a need for cash to pay taxes, then you need to provide a source of quick cash for the executor to draw on. There are several ways to do this, including insurance or assets that can be converted to cash quickly with no loss of value—a money market mutual fund or treasury bills, for example. The point is, unless you develop a detailed estate plan, you may not recognize and prepare for these or other needs.

A well conceived estate plan helps you to make sure certain desirable events occur and certain undesirable alternatives do not occur.

Without a plan someone else—someone you may never have met—could control the disposition of your assets. People you may prefer to exclude might slip in for an undeserved share. Others you would like to see benefit from your money, antiques, and special treasures could be inadvertently left out. Only if you take action while you are living can you be assured that the results you envision will actually take place after your death.

Will You Leave an Estate?

"I don't plan to leave an estate," you might declare. You're not alone. Many people don't see the need to provide for others after their deaths. Mike and Alice S. are proponents of the school of "If I can't take it with me, I'll spend it before I go." Mike wasn't a bit bashful about his estate plan:

"I have left a living trust with all of my assets in it. But that doesn't mean I plan to leave my two sons and my five grandchildren the fruits of my life's work. No way! I earned that money. My wife spent my earnings frugally during the early years when we were building our business and collecting assets. We cut back on our spending and harbored our resources during the time we sent Tom and Eddie to college. They did well in school, and Tom went on to medical school. I have no regrets; in fact, I'm delighted that he had the motivation to hang on through all of those years of internship, residency, then two more years for surgery. He is doing well financially and is careful with his money, something he learned from me and his mother. Why should I leave him two or three hundred thousand bucks? He doesn't expect it. He has already set up trusts to assure his two daughters' college expenses will be paid.

"Eddie did well in school too and took a master's in computer engineering. I can't believe what they pay these hotshots these days. After their three children were in school, Eddie's wife, Corinne, opened her own gift shop; started on a shoestring. She has too much energy to sit around home. She and Eddie began putting away money in Uniform Gifts to Minors trusts for their two girls and a son to attend college.

"So, you see—they don't need me. I figure Mom and I will travel as far and as wide as our money will take us. I don't want to owe anybody, but I plan to spend it all. Mom and I deserve it!"

While some may feel as Mike and Alice do, other couples or individuals prefer to help their children and grandchildren financially. Not all parents have seen their children surpass them in financial security. They may feel a responsibility for helping their children live better than they did. Some continue to help children who find themselves in debt or are unable to help their own children attend college. Whether you prefer to spend your own resources or to leave a stake for children and grandchildren, an estate plan is the essential tool to make sure it happens.

Your estate—that is, everything you own—may be so little that your estate plan can be simple, or even ignored. See Chapters 3 and 4 for guidelines on whether your estate may be too small to matter.

Why You Need an Estate Plan

Most of us prefer to push the thought of our mortality deep into the recesses of our minds. Yet nothing is more certain than death. Shocking as it may seem, we know nothing about and retain only scanty control over how long we may live on this earth. Accidents, strokes, and other sudden fatal occurrences happen to people every day. These thoughts are not intended to scare you but to motivate you to consider an estate plan.

If you say, "I'll take care of it when I'm older," you may be doing yourself and your family a disservice. The price of delay could be disastrous for those you leave behind. As much as half of one's assets may be consumed during the process of conveying the property of a **decedent**—the person who has died—to legal heirs unless action has been taken to provide a plan.

An estate plan should be written to clarify how you would dispose of your assets if you were to die now—today. You can and should review your estate plan every few years to make sure it reflects your current net worth and the latest tax codes. Your plans for conveying your property may change as your family expands, siblings die, parents need care, or federal or state tax laws change. Any number of events may lead to possible estate plan revisions. But your first step is to develop an estate plan that could go into effect tomorrow if it were to become necessary. There are, therefore, two simple reasons for planning your estate—control and cost.

Control

Everyone has a will—of sorts. If you should die **intestate**, that is, without a valid will or a living trust that becomes irrevocable at your death, the state where you live has already written a will for you. A typical state statute that provides for succession is shown in the box on page 14. These state code provisions are "one size fits all," which means they seldom fit anyone exactly. State provisions are written into codes because some order must be brought to the distribution of a decedent's property.

The problems with state codes can be seen in the example of clearing the title of a house. Suppose you and your spouse own your house jointly. Your spouse will inherit full and clear title to the house at your death, and no problem ensues. But at the second death, the property remains on record in your names until some legal action transfers title to another person or institution. If you have a will, it will be presented to **probate court**, which has the responsibility for conveying the property of decedents to heirs in accordance with the laws of the state. The title certifying ownership of the house will be transferred by probate court order. The house now legally belongs to the person or institution you designated when you wrote your will. A similar change of ownership may be effected with a **living**

HOW A STATE CODE MIGHT DISPOSE OF YOUR ESTATE

When a person dies intestate, each state provides a legal succession route for disposal of that person's assets. A typical code provision may read:

1. When a widow (or widower) survives and there is no surviving kin or relatives, the entire estate goes to her (or him).

2. When a widow (or widower) survives and there are children, the surviving spouse takes one-half of the entire estate. The remaining half is divided equally among the children.

3. When a widow (or widower) survives and there are no children but there are other kin, the surviving spouse gets the entire estate up to $50,000. For estates valued in excess of $50,000, the surviving spouse gets $50,000 plus one-half of the remaining personal property and real estate. The remainder is divided as noted in Paragraph No. 5 (below).

4. When neither spouse survives but there are surviving children, all of the estate is divided equally among the children. If one of the children has died, that portion goes to his or her · children. If the deceased child has no children or all of his or her children are deceased, the remaining children divide the estate. If all of the children of the decedent are dead, the estate is divided equally among the grandchildren.

5. If neither spouse survives and there are no children or the decedent is unmarried, the mother and father of the decedent each get one-half of the estate. If either mother or father is dead, all of the estate goes to the survivor. If both mother and father are dead, the estate is divided equally among any brothers or sisters, with their shares to their children (the nephews and nieces) if any brother or sister predeceases the decedent. If no brothers or sisters or children of deceased brothers or sisters are living, then the next of kin inherit in equal amounts. If there are no kin, all goes to the state (this is known as escheat).

---

trust, a specific form of trust that is revocable during the lifetime of the person arranging the trust but becomes irrevocable at that person's death. If you did not write a will or set up a living trust, the state provides a mechanism for transferring legal title to your house and other property to a person or persons designated in the code. You can give your son or daughter your silver service with an informal note. But a family cannot get together and distribute your belongings if they require a legal change of ownership, as with a house or other real property. Only you can make provision for this transfer.

Cost

Shrinkage is the term most planners apply to the costs for settling an estate. Two major costs plus other minor costs can reduce the size of your estate before it is distributed to heirs—the two major costs are taxes and attorney's fees. A well prepared estate plan can minimize both.

Fees For probating a valid will, attorney's fees may range from a few thousand dollars to several million, depending on the size of the estate. Fees may be a flat figure or a percentage of the gross value of the estate, typically 6 to 10 percent. For an estate valued at $100,000, an 8-percent attorney's fees would be $8,000—regardless of the time or work needed to settle the estate. Fees for a million dollar estate could easily amount to $60,000–$70,000. Attorney's fees vary widely from state to state. Of all 50 states, costs for probating a will are probably least in the State of Washington. (See Table 1A for the results of a survey of attorney's fees according to the size of the estate.) An abortive attempt to develop a uniform probate code that would simplify probate court procedures and reduce costs has met with only a lukewarm reception in those states where probate court has been and continues to be a lucrative business for attorneys.

Legal fees associated with settling the estate of someone who dies intestate can be 10 to 20 percent higher than the cost of settling an estate in accordance with provisions of a valid will. To satisfy the probate court in an intestate action, an administrator, accountant, and **appraiser** appointed by the court must be paid in addition to the attorney. An appraiser is a person skilled in placing a value on property. He or she may be licensed or a member of a professional organization of appraisers. A will eliminates some or all of these extra costs.

In addition to a lawyer, an accountant may be required to figure the value of the gross estate and to file an estate tax return with both federal and state governments. These costs will be paid out of the gross estate before assets are distributed. Certified public accountants (CPA) usually work on an hourly basis rather than a percentage of the gross estate, but those charges can be substantial if records are scattered, missing, or controversial. Having a will permits the executor to pick the accountant who may be familiar with the records. A court appointed accountant will not have prior knowledge of the decedent's affairs.

Not so apparent as attorney and accountant fees are the losses that can occur during the lengthy delays that sometimes string out a probate case for years. Assets may be held in a savings account paying a minimum

---

TABLE 1A—ATTORNEY'S FEES*

Sample of Probate Cases From Three Cities (1985)

Estate Value	San Diego, CA	Wilmington, DE	Milwaukee, WI
$80,000–$100,000	$2,182	$1,547	$1,666
$60,000–$80,000	1,798	1,358	1,505
Less than $60,000	1,385	1,285	1,334

NOTE: Arithmetic mean was used to calculate amounts.

*AARP—A Report on Probate—Consumer Perspectives and Concerns, Consumer Affairs Section, 1909 K St., N.W., Washington, DC 20049.

rate of interest, stock values may drop as companies fail or falling earnings depress share prices, and real estate may be held while the market declines. Until the probate court acts, assets cannot be managed to reduce losses or increase value; they remain in limbo. A valid will can shorten the time spent in probate court and allow assets to be released for timely management.

One increasingly popular alternative to a will and the inevitable, costly probate process is the living trust. The bottom line for the decision to go with a will or living trust is—living trusts cost less.

Taxes   Another cost to be managed is taxes. You should be aware of the need for early action if you are to take full advantage of the federal exemptions available. One possible calamity is the loss of a $600,000 exemption (equal to a tax of $192,800) if your and your spouse's taxable estate exceeds $1.2 million. And since state estate or inheritance levies are often based on federal estate returns, you could lose another substantial sum in state taxes if you fail to provide for a tax-saving trust in a will or living trust.

Other Benefits of an Estate Plan

Reduce Delays   Even more frustrating than the shrinkage of an estate's value can be the months the estate is in probate court while the details of a settlement are laboriously resolved. There is little motivation for speedy settlement in probate court even with a valid will. But the delays are even greater in the settlement of the estate of a decedent who has died intestate. The probate court, in its infinite desire to assure a fair and equitable settlement for everyone concerned and to make sure its handling of each case is blameless, drags out the proceedings with administrators and appraisers and continuances. A year is not an unusual time for a will to wend its way through probate. Estate settlements can go on for years if the IRS disagrees with some of the proceedings or if disagreements among heirs must be resolved before final judgment. A challenged will may hang on even longer. In the meantime heirs may have little or no money to live on while the probate court spins its wheels.

Although simpler to resolve, a living trust can still take many months to be settled if the trustee is a bank, attorney, or someone with little motivation to settle amicably and quickly. The main benefit of the living trust is its complete avoidance of the probate court. (See Chapter 5 for a fuller discussion of living trusts.)

Appointment of a Guardian   Some people equate estate planning with retirement. This attitude could be a mistake for a couple with young children. If you make no provisions for the care of a minor, whether your own child or a family member whose responsibility you assume, then all sorts of troubles may crop up. If both parents should be killed in an accident, minor children may live with a brother, sister, grandparents, or a friend. But unless you declare that decision formally in a will (you cannot appoint a guardian through a living trust), a court will decide who, in its opinion, is best suited to bring up your children. More than one row among relatives has erupted in court hearings when guardianship is being considered. A guardian is a person legally responsible for raising a minor.

You might arrange for a brother or sister to take care of your minor children in case you and your spouse should die before the children reach their majority, age 18 in most states. Be sure to ask for the approval of the potential guardian(s), as the responsibility for raising one or more children to adulthood is one a person might not wish to accept. An informal, undocumented arrangement works if the new substitute parents accept the responsibility and little or no money changes hands. However, if other relatives challenge the arrangement, the matter could end up in court. If you prepare for such a contingency and name a guardian for your minor children in a will, a court would not likely change your decision.

Managing an estate for minor children differs from being a guardian. You wouldn't want to saddle a guardian who has agreed to care for your children with the added chore of managing the children's financial affairs. Such a responsibility would entail returning regularly to the court for approval of plans for spending money to support the children. These requests can be time consuming, expensive, and frustrating.

Setting up a trust to provide money for the care of minor children separates the tasks of caring for the children and providing for their financial support. The trust can hold title to the assets, and the trustee can provide money to the guardians for the children's support. When the youngest child attains majority or at some later specified time, such as when he or she reaches age 25 or 30, any remaining assets in the trust can be dispersed to all the children according to provisions of the trust. A trustee managing such a trust need not account to a court for all expenses and/or investment decisions, as he or she functions in a fiduciary capacity.

This freedom to act saves both time and money that could otherwise reduce the funds available for the care and education of the children.

Thus, providing for minor children in case of a catastrophic event that takes the lives of both parents calls for two actions:

• Appointing a guardian to assume personal care for the children.

• Establishing a trust and appointing a trustee to manage the assets you may leave to provide funds to the guardian for support of your children.

Don't attempt to combine both functions within the guardian's responsibilities.

Appointing an Executor or Trustee   An executor is the person you designate to manage the settlement of your estate. (If the person designated is a woman, she may be called an executrix.) The term, personal representative, may also be used to designate the person responsible for handling your estate. Some person or institution will manage the myriad details, both personal and legal, involved in winding up your affairs, and if you fail to write a will or set up a living trust before you die, the probate court will likely appoint an administrator.

Many of the duties of the administrator are similar to those of the executor except that the administrator must account for his actions to the probate court. The administrator may be a family member or someone who may not know you and your heirs. He or she will proceed to process the assets in your estate in accordance with the state's laws of succession for persons who die intestate. To protect him or herself from possible suits and to assure all details are fully documented, he may rely more on accountants and appraisers than an executor. This invariably increases the cost of settling an estate.

Availing yourself of the opportunity to appoint an executor can be a plus or a minus depending on how you make your choice. On the plus side you can pick a person you trust, who knows you and your family, and who may serve without a bond. Not having to satisfy the bonding requirement saves money. Unless you specify that the executor may serve without a bond, the court will probably saddle your executor with this cost.

On the minus side, an inexperienced executor could cost you more than you think. Failing to act promptly or to file timely tax returns can lead to needless penalties. A spouse appointed to be an executor or executrix may rely on specialists, attorneys, or accountants, but costs may increase. If the executor is not an accomplished money manager, opportunities for expanding the value of assets may be lost or mishandled.

Selecting an executor calls for serious thought. Avoid sentimentality in picking a person to manage your estate. Remember two things:

• An executor may be held liable to the beneficiaries and/or creditors of an estate for losses resulting from his or her actions. The executor may be the subject of suits by disenchanted legatees or held personally liable for acts of omission or commission.

• Any actions the executor takes can not benefit him. His fiduciary responsibility calls for keeping the estate whole.

Since the executor appears to have everything to lose and is prevented from gaining any benefits, he or she can be in an unenviable position. Bearing in mind this no-win situation, make sure the executor you pick is willing and able to serve. An executor does not serve free; he or she is entitled to compensation.

If, after considering these facts, you still elect to appoint a spouse or one of your adult children to be the executor of your estate, at least consider the appointment of a co-executor. This person should have experience and expertise in the settlement of estates and the management of money. Your instructions to the family member should be to seek counsel as early as possible following a funeral or memorial service. Management of one's estate requires knowledgeable, professional attention.

In addition to the appointment of an executor or co-executor, consider a successor executor. The successor executor picks up the reins if the executor you appoint refuses to act, is not available, or has died. If you decide on a family member or friend to be an executor and that person declines or is not available, a corporate executor, such as the trust department of a bank, may be named.

Caring for a Disabled Dependent   Closely allied with appointing a guardian and financial manager for minor children is the issue of caring for someone who is disabled and unable to care for himself or herself. A child may be profoundly retarded or afflicted with some permanent disability that would prevent the child being either self-supporting or able to care for himself or herself. An aging parent may be financially dependent on your resources either while living in your home or in a retirement community or nursing home. A close relative may have been injured so severely in an accident that he or she requires long-term care or cannot be self-supporting.

Whatever the reason for dependency, you may now be providing care and/or support from your current income or other assets, possibly an insurance settlement following disablement in an accident. Question: what would happen to the disabled and/or dependent person if you should no longer be around to pick up the tab for support or manage the person's assets? If you should die intestate, a court ordered distribution of your assets might not include the one person most desperately in need of continued support. A testamentary trust set up in a will and that goes into effect when the will is probated could provide continued support for the handicapped person or dependent. These dependents must be identified and the level of support you envision for them must be specified while you are living.

Dispensing of Jointly Owned Property

You may own some property, such as your personal residence, jointly with your spouse. When spouses own their home jointly, the surviving spouse ends up with clear title to the house when the other spouse dies. But when the surviving spouse dies, a will or living trust is needed to dispose of property that was once jointly owned. Owning a house jointly does not avoid probate, for example; it only postpones probate until the death of the second spouse.

A surviving spouse with clear title to his or her home may change the arrangement to joint ownership with a son or daughter to avoid probate. But if such an action is taken out of the context of a well conceived estate plan, numerous problems for heirs could result (see Chapter 7). You could substitute another joint owner in your estate plan if you wish to keep the action out of probate court.

Conclusion

Consider an estate plan as insurance. The plan can help to protect your interests at death and probably reduce costs and delays to a minimum.

Yet in addition to obstacles we've already discussed, two other considerations may be preventing you from preparing an estate plan. First, many people are intimidated by lawyers. Admittedly, lawyers can sometimes appear brusque—even unhelpful. But not all attorneys are unapproachable. They provide a needed service, and you should learn to work with them. Second, costs associated with drafting a will or a living trust may cause you to postpone action. But, the costs of not having a will or living trust can be far greater. You cannot afford not to have some plan in place. Even the simplest of wills drawn by a store-front legal clinic may be preferable to no will at all. Custom drafted wills or living trusts will cost more, but their benefits far exceed their costs.

The following chapters detail the many paths to be traveled in developing your estate plan. Use this information to help you in your own thinking:

• Who will be your heirs?

• Should you set up a will or a living trust?

• How much will estate and/or inheritance taxes reduce the value of your estate?

• Who will manage your estate?

Remember that when it comes to drawing up the final documents, you will need the help of a professional. But careful consideration of these and other factors detailed in the following chapters will reduce the time needed for an attorney to draft a will or develop a living trust document. And saving time with an attorney reduces the cost of implementing your estate plan.

CHAPTER TWO

Sizing Up Your Estate

KEY TERMS IN THIS CHAPTER

net worth	*inheritance tax*
gross estate	*tax-saving trust*
liability	*capitalization*
taxable estate	*personal property*

The value of your property in dollar terms has an enormous effect on how you plan your estate. If all of your property, personal and real, totals less than $30,000 ($60,000 in some states), you may not need a formal estate plan. If you own property worth more than this, you can benefit from a plan for conveying it equitably and inexpensively to your children or other heirs.

How much do you own? Surprisingly few people can place a figure on their **net worth**; that is, the dollar value of their assets minus their liabilities. In other words, your net worth is how much you own less how much you owe.

Many people significantly underestimate the value of their assets. You may, for instance, have developed a statement of net worth, either as a preliminary step for seeking a loan or as a regular step in man-aging your money. But while it is a step in the right direction, a statement of net worth seldom values your property in enough detail to serve in developing an estate plan.

An estate plan is based on your **gross estate**, the total value of all your property and belongings. A statement of net worth may not include the death benefits available on your life insurance, but your gross estate would include them. Property you may be carrying on your statement of net worth at cost will be boosted to the fair market value when compiling your gross estate. On the other hand, personal property, such as furniture, luggage, an electric shaver and the myriad other tools, accessories, and miscellany that helps you live more comfortably, may be excluded from your gross estate valuation or valued far below their usefulness.

Calculating Your Tax Liability

Potential estate tax **liability** is the driving force behind knowing how much your estate is worth. Two values are important: your gross estate and your **taxable estate**. This is your gross estate less all debts, expenses (including attorney, accountant, and appraiser fees), and probate court costs, if any.

The size of your estate will dictate how you form your estate plan to minimize your tax liability. Different values call for different strategies. Here are four major variables affecting your tax situation:

• If you are single and your taxable estate totals less than $600,000, you will owe no federal estate tax. Since many states levy an estate or **inheritance tax** based on a federal estate return, you may owe no state taxes either.

• If you are single and the value of your taxable estate exceeds $600,000, you may need to take some specific action to reduce or eliminate your potential tax liability.

• If you are married and your taxable estate totals less than $1.2 million, you may or may not be liable for federal estate taxes after the death of one spouse, depending on how you plan your estate. If, for example, your estate plan includes a **tax-saving trust**, no federal estate taxes will be due at the death of the second spouse unless the value of the estate has escalated since the first spouse's death.

• If you are married and your taxable estate exceeds $1.2 million, you definitely need a plan to help minimize your estate's potential tax liabilities. Alternative strategies are available if you plan well.

How Big Is Your Estate?

How big is your estate? You reach this all-important dollar figure by working through all of the numbers that affect property you own. The worksheets on pages 23–43 will help you first, to identify the property you own and second, to put a realistic value on it. Like a statement of net worth, this estate valuation represents a snapshot of your estate's worth at a given moment in time. Essentially, it answers the question—"What is my gross estate worth today?" Next week you could inherit a house. Or the value of one or more of your stock holdings could balloon at any time. Any number of events could change the value of your estate next week, next month, or next year, but you still need to calculate your gross estate's value as of today. Then, you should plan regular updates of your estate valuation to keep abreast of any impact a higher gross estate may have on your planning. You should follow outside events that impact on your gross estate as well. For instance, the current exemption of $600,000 net taxable assets per person protects a substantial portion of many estates from taxes. However, the protective value of this exemption could be swiftly eroded by a boom in real estate prices, an escalation of stock prices, or inflation in general. Congress is also considering a change that would lower the exemption. Furthermore, if you are sitting on an estate currently valued at $400,000, it could easily double within 15 years even if inflation averages only 5 percent—the approximate current rate. This increase would push you over the limit of $600,000.

Knowing the taxable value of your estate and how it would be taxed is important because the first dollar over the exemption level will be taxed by the federal government at 37 percent. The 37-percent rate is the marginal estate tax rate. A regular updating of your appraisal of the value of your gross estate will keep you apprised of a need for changes in your estate plan.

How to Begin Calculating Your Taxable Estate

The worksheets on pages 23–38 aim to find the total value of your property—your estate's gross value. Administrative and legal expenses, outstanding debts, probate costs, if any, and local taxes will reduce your gross estate to a taxable estate. This is the important value because it is this figure that affects how much of your estate is exempted and how much tax you will have to pay.

Compiling Values For Your Gross Estate Information is the key. Don't expect to create or make changes in your estate plan on rough estimates. Figure the value of your estate as accurately as possible.

A walk-through of the summary form (Worksheet 2A), for your taxable estate on pages 23–27 will help you assemble the facts you need. Begin with "Assets-Liquid"; these are assets that can be immediately accessed, for example by writing a check on your checking account. You need to pick a date that will be the snapshot date. All of the evaluations must be related to that date to assure comparable data. To simplify collection of such data as the balance in a money market mutual fund, you could pick the last day of a quarter. Confirmations are typically sent by mutual funds to reflect balances at the end of each quarter.

WORKSHEET 2A—Summary of Your Taxable Estate

ASSETS

Liquid		Amount
1. Cash—Checking Acct. #1		_____
Checking Acct. #2		
2. Savings— Bank #1		_____
Bank #2		
3. Savings— Credit Union		_____
4. Money Market Mutual Fund (Name)		_____
" " " " (Name)		_____
" " " " (Name)		_____
" " " " (Name)		_____
Subtotal Liquid Assets		_____

(continued on next page)

ASSETS (Cont.)

Near Liquid (Withdrawable)

    1. Cash value— Life Insurance #1 _____

                 "   "   "   "   #2 _____

                 "   "   "   "   #3 _____

    2. Broker's Account #1 _____

             "   "   #2 _____

    3. U.S. Treasury Bills _____

         "   "   Notes _____

         "   "   Bonds _____

    4. Other _____

                            Subtotal Near Liquid Assets _____

                            Total Liquid Assets _____

Marketable Investments   **Market Value (Date)**

    1. Common Stocks (Worksheet 2A-1) _____

    2. Preferred Stocks (Worksheet 2A-2) _____

    3. Bonds—Taxable (Worksheet 2A-3) _____

    4.   "   —Municipal (Worksheet 2A-4) _____

    5. Mutual Funds (Worksheet 2A-5) _____

    6. Other _____

                   Subtotal Marketable Investments _____

Unmarketable Investments

1. Limited Partnerships (Worksheet 2A-6) _____

2. Business Partnership Interest _____

3. " Ownership _____

4. Vested Profit Sharing _____

5. " Pension Benefit or Keogh _____

6. " 401(k) Savings _____

7. " 403(B) " _____

8. IRA _____

9. Real Estate (Worksheet 2A-7) _____

10. Notes Receivable (Worksheet 2A-8) _____

11. Trust(s) _____

12. Life Insurance Death Benefits (Worksheet 2A-9) _____

Subtotal Unmarketable Investments _____

Personal Property **Current Value***

Automobiles, Boat, Sports Equip. (Worksheet 2A-10) _____

Household Goods (Worksheet 2A-11) _____

Jewelry, Furs, etc. (Worksheet 2A-12) _____

Collections, Hobby Equipment (Worksheet 2A-13) _____

Antiques (Worksheet 2A-14) _____

Electronics (Worksheet 2A-15) _____

Other (Worksheet 2A-16) _____

Subtotal Personal Property _____

TOTAL ASSETS _____

*Current value may be depreciated, appraised market, or estimated fair market value depending on item(s).

(continued on next page)

LIABILITIES

Current Bills	**Amount**
Monthly Charge Accounts (Worksheet 2A-17)	_____
Doctor, Hospital, Dental Bills (Worksheet 2A-18)	_____
Utilities (Worksheet 2A-19)	_____
Other	_____
Subtotal Current Bills	_____

Installment Debts	
Auto, Boat, Sports Equip. (Worksheet 2A-20)	_____
Finance Company Loan	_____
Insurance Policy Loan(s) (Worksheet 2A-21)	_____
Credit Union Loan	_____
Furniture, Appliance, Electronics (Worksheet 2A-22)	_____
Notes Payable (Worksheet 2A-23)	_____
Other	_____
Subtotal Installment Debt	_____

Long Term Debt	
Mortgage Loans (Worksheet 2A-24)	_____
Land Contract	_____
Other	_____
Subtotal Long Term Debt	_____

Taxes	Amount
Income—Federal	_____
" —State	_____
Real Estate	_____
Personal Property	_____
Other	_____
Subtotal Taxes	_____
TOTAL LIABILITIES	_____
GROSS ESTATE VALUATION	_____
Assets	_____
Liabilities	_____
TOTAL GROSS ESTATE VALUATION	_____

ESTATE SETTLEMENT EXPENSES**	_____
Executor Expenses	_____
Attorney Fees	_____
Accountant	_____
Appraiser	_____
Other	_____
TOTAL SETTLEMENT EXPENSES	_____

TAXABLE ESTATE VALUATION	_____
Gross Estate Valuation	_____
Expenses	_____
TOTAL TAXABLE ESTATE	_____

**Estimates where necessary.

On your snapshot date, look at your check register to get the uncommitted total of checking accounts No. 1 and 2. If you have only one, obviously, leave the second blank. Check your bank for the up-to-the-minute balance of any savings accounts. Call your credit union, if you have one, for a similar balance.

Near liquid assets are accessible but only with some difficulty; that is, you can't simply write a check. Rather than sift through your life insurance policies, ask your broker for help in finding the current cash value of your life insurance policies. If you deal with a stockbroker, you may retain a credit or margin account balance. Call to find this account number from whatever brokers you do business with. U.S. Treasury securities accrue interest each day. They also move up and down in value in accordance with the general interest environment. The simplest way to calculate the value of Treasury bills

---

WORKSHEET 2A-1

COMMON STOCKS

Name	No. of Shares	Cost Basis	Current Market Value
1. _____	_____	_____	_____
2. _____	_____	_____	_____
3. _____	_____	_____	_____
4. _____	_____	_____	_____
5. _____	_____	_____	_____
6. _____	_____	_____	_____
7. _____	_____	_____	_____
8. _____	_____	_____	_____
9. _____	_____	_____	_____
10. _____	_____	_____	_____
11. _____	_____	_____	_____
12. _____	_____	_____	_____
		TOTAL	_____

WORKSHEET 2A-2

PREFERRED STOCKS

Name	No. of Shares	Cost Basis	Current Market Value
1. _____	_____	_____	_____
2. _____	_____	_____	_____
3. _____	_____	_____	_____
4. _____	_____	_____	_____
5. _____	_____	_____	_____
		TOTAL	_____

WORKSHEET 2A-3

BONDS—Taxable

Name	Face Amount	Cost Basis	Percent Yield	Maturity Date	Current Market Value
1._____	_____	_____	_____	_____	_____
2._____	_____	_____	_____	_____	_____
3._____	_____	_____	_____	_____	_____
4._____	_____	_____	_____	_____	_____
5._____	_____	_____	_____	_____	_____
6._____	_____	_____	_____	_____	_____
7._____	_____	_____	_____	_____	_____
8. U.S. Savings Bonds	_____	_____	_____	_____	_____
				TOTAL	_____

WORKSHEET 2A-4

BONDS—Municipal

Name	Face Amount	Cost Basis	Percent Yield	Maturity Date	Current Market Value
1.					
2.					
3.					
4.					
5.					
6.					
7.					
8.					
				TOTAL	

WORKSHEET 2A-5

MUTUAL FUNDS (Except Money Market Funds)

Name	No. of Shares	Cost Basis	Current Market Value
1.			
2.			
3.			
4.			
5.			
6.			
7.			
8.			
9.			
10.			
	TOTAL		

WORKSHEET 2A-6

LIMITED PARTNERSHIP(S)

Program Name	Amount Invested	Expected Maturity	Estimated Cash-Out Value
1. _____	_____	_____	_____
2. _____	_____	_____	_____
3. _____	_____	_____	_____

WORKSHEET 2A-7

REAL ESTATE

Item	Original Investment	Capital Improvements	Cost Basis	Current Net Market Value*
Personal Residence	_____	_____	_____	_____
Vacation Place	_____	_____	_____	_____
Rental House/Condo	_____	_____	_____	_____
Time-Share	_____	_____	_____	_____
			TOTAL	_____

*Gross market value less selling and closing costs

WORKSHEET 2A-8

NOTES RECEIVABLE

Name	Face Amount	Interest Rate	Maturity Date	Current Value
1.				
2.				
3.				
4.				
5.				
TOTAL				

(T-bills) is to calculate the accrued interest with the assumption that you will hold them to maturity. For example, if your snapshot date is September 30 and you own three-month T-bills due to mature on October 31, you have owned them for two of the three months. Add two-thirds of the difference between the price you paid and their maturity value to the price paid to reach a current value on September 30. Suppose you paid $9,812.50 on August 1 for one T-bill that will pay you $10,000 at maturity on October 31. Two months have elapsed since the purchase, so you have earned two-thirds of the $187.50 difference between the purchase price of $9,812.50 and the maturity value of $10,000. Accrued interest would amount to $125.00. Thus, the value of the T-bill on September 30 equals $9,812.50 plus $125.00 or $9,937.50. Treasury notes and bonds pay interest at the rate stated on the bonds twice yearly. Either check *The Wall Street Journal* the next day after your snapshot date for a quote on the notes or bonds, or call your broker. Add the accrued interest from the date of the last payment. You can do this by calculating the daily interest and multiplying that rate by the number of days from the last payment date to your snapshot date.

Calculate the net market value of marketable securities according to the Worksheets 2A-1 through 2A-5 and bring the totals into the lines on the summary. Complete the line items for unmarketable investments (limited partnerships) on Worksheet 2A-6. Compile asset values for real estate and notes receivable on Worksheets 2A-7 and 2A-8 respectively. Life insurance death benefits (Worksheet 2A-9) include the face value plus any dividends left with the policy. Ask your agent for help. See below for ideas to help you estimate the value of personal property to complete the listing of assets.

As you collect the various numbers for different parts of the estate valuation (Worksheets 2A-1 through 2A-16), you will find that the figures you put down offer different degrees of accuracy. Some figures are precise. For example, you can check the closing prices of any stocks you may own any day exchanges are open and come up with a specific dollar valuation.

Other property, however, may call for estimates or judgment. Your biggest asset may be your home (see Worksheet 2A–7). How much it is worth depends on the market value less settlement costs. Basically, a house is worth whatever a buyer is willing to pay and a seller is willing to accept. Real estate agents typically estimate a high market value for a house. A tax assessor will likely place a value considerably under the market value of your house. Even a professional appraiser must rely somewhat on

---

WORKSHEET 2A-9

LIFE INSURANCE DEATH BENEFITS

Policy	Face Value	Dividend Accruals	Cash Value*	Current Benefit Value
1. Cash Value Policy	_____	_____	_____	_____
2. " " "	_____	_____	_____	_____
3. " " "	_____	_____	_____	_____
4. " " "	_____	_____	_____	_____
5. " " "	_____	_____	_____	_____
6. Term Policy	_____	_____	_____	_____
7. " "	_____	_____	_____	_____
8. " "	_____	_____	_____	_____
9. Group Policy (Work)	_____	_____	_____	_____
10. Group Policy (Work)	_____	_____	_____	_____
			TOTAL	_____

*Deduct cash value from benefit value to avoid double counting—See Cash Values in ASSETS—Near Liquid.

WORKSHEET 2A-10

AUTO, BOAT, SPORTS EQUIPMENT

Item	Original Cost	Current Value*
1. Auto #1	_____	_____
2. Auto #2	_____	_____
3. Other vehicle**	_____	_____
4. Boat #1	_____	_____
5. Boat #2	_____	_____
6. Skis (All Family)	_____	_____
7. Exercise Equipment	_____	_____
8. Fishing Gear (Rods, etc.)	_____	_____
9. Hunting Gear (Guns, etc.)	_____	_____
10. _____	_____	_____
TOTAL		_____

*Dollar value—Appraised, depreciated or market
**Motorcycle, moped, snowmobile, or other

---

judgment, experience, values of comparable houses in the neighborhood, and perceptions. While none of these attempts to value your house will be as precise as your valuation of a stock holding, get the best value you can to plug into that part of your worksheet, recognizing that some level of inaccuracy is inevitable.

Land and investment real estate call for the same sort of evaluation. Land without improvements can be particularly difficult to evaluate since its worth depends on what the person owning or buying it will do with it and any zoning regulations that may limit its use. But do the best you can, recognizing that its value could escalate with time. Rental houses may provide an income stream. Their value may be more easily estimated from the **capitalization** of that income stream, a method of valuing real estate based on its earning capacity. A capitalization rate of 10 percent means the price or capital value is 10 times the annual income. You might consult with a real estate agent dealing in commercial property.

Calling for even more subjective judgments are valuations of **personal property**; that is property you own other than real estate, such as a car, clothing, furniture, jewelry, and appliances (see Worksheets 2A-10–16). Attempting to place a value on personal property for an estate valuation is similar to the problem of developing a statement of net worth. Jewelry can be appraised by a jeweler or collector, for example. Collections, such as a stamp album, antique cars, old firearms, baseball cards, coins, or any of many specialties vary widely in value according to who is appraising them. Recognize, too, that the appraised value of an antique chest, for example, will not be the price you could necessarily get for it. If an antique chest is appraised at $10,000, you or the person who inherits it might get only 50 percent of its appraised value, or $5,000, in a sale to a dealer or at an auction. But the "fair market value" is the $10,000 figure and is the one you should note on the worksheet.

Furniture, furnishings, and clothing are obviously valuable to you, but they can be worth much less in an evaluation for estate purposes. Realistically, you should tabulate the depreciated value of such items. If, for example, you bought a chair for $100 and you expect it to serve you for 10 years, depreciate it at $10 per year. If you have

---

WORKSHEET 2A-11

HOUSEHOLD GOODS

Item	Original Cost	Current Value
1. Furniture	_____	_____
2. Appliances	_____	_____
3. Lawn Equipment (Mower, etc.)	_____	_____
4. Oriental Rugs	_____	_____
5. Silver (Flatware & Holloware)	_____	_____
6. China	_____	_____
7. Kitchen Equipment	_____	_____
8. Personal Clothing*	_____	_____
9. _____	_____	_____
10. _____	_____	_____
	TOTAL	_____

*Includes only items with market value, e.g., women's dresses sold in second-hand shops

WORKSHEET 2A-12

JEWELRY, FURS, ETC.

Item	Original Cost	Current Value*
1. _____	_____	_____
2. _____	_____	_____
3. _____	_____	_____
4. _____	_____	_____
5. _____	_____	_____
6. _____	_____	_____
7. _____	_____	_____
8. _____	_____	_____
9. _____	_____	_____
10. _____	_____	_____
TOTAL		_____

*Fair market value

WORKSHEET 2A-13

COLLECTIONS, HOBBY EQUIPMENT

Item	Original Cost	Current Value*
1. Camera(s)	_____	_____
2. Stamp Collection	_____	_____
3. Coin Collection	_____	_____
4. Other Collection	_____	_____
5. Workship Equipment	_____	_____
6. Other TOTAL		_____

*Appraised, depreciated, or fair market value

WORKSHEET 2A-14

ANTIQUES

Item	Fair Market Value
1. _____	_____
2. _____	_____
3. _____	_____
4. _____	_____
5. _____	_____
6. _____	_____
7. _____	_____
8. _____	_____
TOTAL	_____

WORKSHEET 2A-15

ELECTRONICS

Item	Original Cost	Current Value*
1. Television #1	_____	_____
2. " #2	_____	_____
3. VCR(s)	_____	_____
4. Camcorder	_____	_____
5. Computer	_____	_____
6. Other	TOTAL	_____

*Appraised, depreciated, or fair market value

WORKSHEET 2A-16

OTHER PERSONAL PROPERTY

Item	Original Cost	Current Value
1. Livestock	_____	_____
2. Patent(s)	_____	_____
3. Copyrights	_____	_____
4. Paintings	_____	_____
5. Other art	_____	_____
6. _____	_____	_____
7. _____	_____	_____
8. _____	_____	_____
TOTAL		_____

---

owned it for five years when you are compiling values for the worksheet, put it down as worth $50. While such a process may build in a bias for a higher price than could be realized in an estate sale or sale to a dealer, it will help you complete the evaluation with some consistency.

Compiling Liabilities　How much you owe; that is, your liabilities, can be compiled more precisely than how much you own (see Worksheets 2A-17–24). Compiling your liabilities will also be easier if you pick the end of a month as your snapshot date. Separate worksheets generate single figures you enter on the summary. A finance company loan will include the remaining balance due plus any accrued interest. Your account payment book will provide the numbers you need. Calculate the current amount due on a credit union loan the same way.

Generally, you can work from amortization schedules for real estate debt and statements received monthly. Remember, the estate valuation represents a snapshot of your financial position at an instant in time. If you intend to pay $1,000 on your bank card statement next week, you may write a check on your account at the bank. Paying off a bill has no effect on total valuation: reducing the debt also reduces cash in the

WORKSHEET 2A-17

MONTHLY CHARGE ACCOUNTS

Account	Finance Charges (Rate)	Current Balance
1. Department Store #1	_____	_____
2. " " #2	_____	_____
3. " " #3	_____	_____
4. American Express Card	_____	_____
5. Bank Card #1	_____	_____
6. Bank Card #2	_____	_____
7. Oil Company Credit Card #1	_____	_____
8. " " " " #2	_____	_____
9. Home Equity Loan	_____	_____
10. _____	_____	_____
11. _____	_____	_____
12. _____	_____	_____
	TOTAL	_____

WORKSHEET 2A-18

DOCTOR, HOSPITAL, DENTAL BILLS

Account	Scheduled Monthly Payment	Current Balance
1. Doctor #1	_____	_____
2. " #2	_____	_____
3. Hospital	_____	_____
4. Dentist #1	_____	_____
5. " #2	_____	_____
TOTAL		_____

WORKSHEET 2A-19

UTILITIES

Account	Current Balance
1. Electric Power Co.	_____
2. Water Co.	_____
3. Fuel Dealer or Gas Co.	_____
4. Rubbish Disposal	_____
5. Monitored House Protection	_____
6. Telephone	_____
7. Lawn Maintenance	_____
8. Sewer	_____
9. _____	_____
10. _____	_____
TOTAL	_____

WORKSHEET 2A-20

INSTALLMENT DEBTS

Account/Contract	Monthly Payment	Current Balance
1. Auto #1	_____	_____
2. " #2	_____	_____
3. Other Vehicle*	_____	_____
4. Boat	_____	_____
5. Canoe, Windsurfer or Other	_____	_____
6. Skis	_____	_____
7. Exercise Equipment	_____	_____
8. Sports Equipment	_____	_____
9. _____	_____	_____
10. _____	_____	_____
TOTAL		_____

*Motorcycle, moped, snowmobile, or other

WORKSHEET 2A-21

INSURANCE POLICY LOANS

Policy	Interest Rate	Current Balance
1. Loan Policy #1	_____	_____
2. " " #2	_____	_____
3. " " #3	_____	_____
4. " " #4	_____	_____
TOTAL		_____

WORKSHEET 2A-22

FURNITURE, APPLIANCES, ELECTRONICS

Account	Monthly Payment	Current Balance
1. Furniture Contract #1	_____	_____
2. " " #2	_____	_____
3. Appliance Contract #1	_____	_____
4. " " #2	_____	_____
5. Television Contract	_____	_____
6. Computer Contract	_____	_____
7. Camcorder Contract	_____	_____
8. _____	_____	_____
9. _____	_____	_____
10. _____	_____	_____
TOTAL		_____

---

bank. How much you estimate for current bills for utilities, bank card, and other creditors will have only a minimal effect on how much you owe overall. One exception may be a large medical bill. If you owe several thousand dollars for previous medical or hospital care, that liability will reduce your estate's taxable value. All debts will be paid off by the executor or administrator of your estate prior to figuring any taxes.

All installment debts will be paid from estate funds. Calculate the outstanding account balances of any installment contracts for a car, boat, furniture, or appliances in figuring the gross estate value. If you have borrowed against the cash and accumulated dividend value of your life insurance policies, include all of these account totals. Your life insurance company will deduct all loans before paying out any death benefits due from policies. Include the outstanding balances owned on any credit union, finance company, home equity, or personal loans.

If you are paying on a home loan mortgage, ask your lender for an amortization schedule unless you have one already. Note the outstanding balance remaining according to how many payments you have

WORKSHEET 2A-23

NOTES PAYABLE

Lender	Months Remaining	Monthly Payment	Current Balance
1. Personal Loan —Father	_____	_____	_____
2. " " —Brother	_____	_____	_____
3. Bank Loan	_____	_____	_____
4. Credit Union Loan	_____	_____	_____
5. Finance Company Loan	_____	_____	_____
6. _____	_____	_____	_____
7. _____	_____	_____	_____
8. _____	_____	_____	_____
TOTAL			_____

WORKSHEET 2A-24

MORTGAGE LOANS

	Amortization Schedule		
Lender	Time Remaining	Payment	Current Balance
1. Resident Mortgage Loan	_____	_____	_____
2. Vacation Place " "	_____	_____	_____
3. Rental Property #1	_____	_____	_____
4. " " #2	_____	_____	_____
TOTAL			_____

made. This balance partially offsets the full value of your home noted on the asset side of the estate valuation. Put the current net market value of the house in the asset side and your loan balance on the liability side. The net worth figure will flow into the overall totals automatically. Use a contract payment schedule to find the outstanding balance you may owe on a land or other real estate contract.

Taxes due at death will also reduce the gross value of your estate. Your executor or administrator will use available cash, usually from insurance proceeds, to pay any income taxes due plus any assessments or real estate liabilities that may have accrued or will accrue before the estate is settled and title to property transferred to the new owners. When property title is transferred, the new owners receive the property free of any taxes on the date of transfer. Thus, all taxes due until the date of title transfer remain the responsibility of the estate.

Your net gross estate results from totalling all assets and subtracting all liabilities from the asset total, as shown in Figure 2A.

The final step, calculating your taxable estate, will require estimating expenses for settling the estate. Included among these expenses are attorney, accountant, and appraiser fees plus fees to the executor, if that person is a professional rather than a friend or relative. A number of miscellaneous fees, such as a cost for surveying property, may also boost the total for expenses.

Estimated expenses are just that—estimates. Consult your attorney to ask for his or her estimate for settling the estate. Get similar estimates from your accountant. Potential fees from your executor will depend on who it is; a family member might be willing to serve at no cost to your estate. Otherwise, ask your attorney to estimate the expenses an outside executor might charge. Then, estimate the potential shrinkage. (See Chapters 4 and 5.) At this point you can decide on an estate plan that will minimize expenses. But unless you work through the numbers, you won't know whether a correction is needed to leave more of an estate for your heirs.

Conclusion

Calculating your taxable estate is the first step in estate planning. Until you know whether you will have to pay taxes, you cannot take those actions needed to assure a speedy, low-cost conveyance of your property to heirs. Although the details of calculating your taxable estate may appear formidable, the old advice of "filling in the blanks one line at a time" still applies. You may find that many of the lines in the worksheet do not apply to your situation. Leave them blank, but look at them carefully—they are there to help you remember.

CHAPTER THREE

Taxes and Costs:
Planning to Minimize Both

KEY TERMS IN THIS CHAPTER

exemption   *pickup tax*
dower interest   *adult adoption*
curtesy interest   *domicile*
marital deduction

Relatively few estates pay federal estate taxes now that the Unified Gift and Estate Tax Schedule is in full effect. In 1981, Congress made major changes in rules and rates in the estate tax code. From 1942 to 1976 the **exemption** from taxes levied on individuals' estates was only $40,000. As a result most people leaving even modest estates at their death also left estate tax liabilities. Wealthy individuals found estate taxes unconscionably high, even "confiscatory." Tax rates on gifts were only 75 percent of the rates on taxable estate assets. The cries finally penetrated the halls of Congress. Exemptions were raised in 1976 and again in 1981 (exemptions apply only to U.S. citizens). Gradually over a five-year period estate and/or gift tax exemptions rose to their present level of $192,800, equivalent to the estate or gift tax on $600,000 of taxable assets. (See Table 3A on page 46 for the current Unified Gift and Estate Tax schedule.) Even though the full credit of $192,800 has been applicable to returns filed for decedents who died after December 31, 1987, inflation has already begun to affect estate taxes. As time goes on and inflation continues its course, the number of estates liable for taxes will probably continue to rise.

The rates in Table 3A apply to United States citizens (even if they reside outside the United States). Different rules apply to surviving spouses who are aliens, even though the estate tax rates remain the same. These differences are detailed and sometimes onerous. If you and/or your spouse are aliens residing in the United States, you need to seek special counsel in planning your estate.

TABLE 3A

Unified Federal Estate and Gift Tax Rate Schedule
U.S. Citizens and Residents

| Taxable Amount Passing— | | Tax Due | |
Over	But not over	Of the excess over	
$0	$10,000	$0 + 18%	$0
$10,000	$20,000	$1,800 + 20%	$10,000
$20,000	$40,000	$3,800 + 22%	$20,000
$40,000	$60,000	$8,200 + 24%	$40,000
$60,000	$80,000	$13,000 + 26%	$60,000
$80,000	$100,000	$18,200 + 28%	$80,000
$100,000	$150,000	$23,800 + 30%	$100,000
$150,000	$250,000	$38,800 + 32%	$150,000
$250,000	$500,000	$70,800 + 34%	$250,000
$500,000	$750,000	$155,800 + 37%	$500,000
$750,000	$1,000,000	$248,300 + 39%	$750,000
$1,000,000	$1,250,000	$345,800 + 41%	$1,000,000
$1,250,000	$1,500,000	$448,300 + 43%	$1,250,000
$1,500,000	$2,000,000	$555,800 + 45%	$1,500,000
$2,000,000	$2,500,000	$780,800 + 49%	$2,000,000
$2,500,000	$3,000,000	$1,025,800 + 53%	$2,500,000
$3,000,000	—	$1,290,000 + 55%	$3,000,000

*There is a 5% surtax on amounts in excess of $10,000,000 but not in excess of $21,040,000 ($18,340,000 after 1992).

Three Possible Taxes on Estates

When you plan your estate, bear in mind that you may face three different types of taxes.

Federal and State Income Taxes

A surviving spouse may file a joint income tax return for the year his or her spouse died. Such returns are no different from joint returns filed during the years both spouses were alive. Total income may be less if the decedent died early in the year and was the primary earner. Income taxes are not levied against assets; that is the arena for estate taxes, if any. However, any capital gains paid to the decedent or spouse will be reported and the joint return should reflect such distributions. Normally, filing a joint return will result in lower taxes but not always. You or your tax advisor should calculate taxes two or possibly three ways to determine the least tax. Of the three taxes possible, paying an income tax on income earned by the decedent is the one you are most likely to face.

Federal Estate Tax

No estate tax is due if the value of your taxable estate falls below $600,000, but your executor may still be required to file Form 706, the Estate Tax Return. Form 706 is not required if your gross estate totals less than $600,000. If you are married and your spouse survives you, an exemption equivalent to $1.2 million of taxable assets is available, providing you take advantage of the tax limiting moves in planning your estate (see below). Note the following quotation from the Tax Court: *"No one has to arrange his or her affairs to satisfy the appetite of the tax collector. However, where a taxpayer has failed to arrange his or her affairs to minimize taxation, they should not expect the Tax Court to do it for them."*

State Estate or Inheritance Taxes

Not all states levy taxes on gifts and/or estates. A number of states have within the past few years legislated an end to these so-called "death taxes." The states of California and Washington, for example, no longer collect an inheritance tax. Nevada collects neither an estate nor inheritance tax. Note the difference: An estate tax is paid by the estate before any assets are distributed to heirs. An inheritance tax is paid by the person receiving the inheritance. In those states that retain an inheritance tax, the exemption and the rate payable on amounts over the exemption will likely be determined by the relationship between the decedent and the heir.

Filing a Federal Estate Tax Return

In the following discussion, the term executor, signifies the person or persons you have named in your will or as successor trustee of your living trust to manage your estate. One of the primary duties of an executor (of a will) or a trustee (of a living trust) is to settle accounts with the Internal Revenue Service representing the United States Treasury. The Estate Tax Return is due nine months after the decedent's death. Numerous problems could delay the timely filing, and an extension of time may be allowed when requested on Form 4768, Application for Extension of Time to File U.S. Estate Tax Return and/or Pay Estate Tax. Approval of this request for an extension of time is not automatic as it often is for federal income tax extension requests. The executor must file the application for extension in plenty of time for the IRS to reply before the deadline for filing. Even if the time for filing is extended, the executor must pay the tax unless a delay in payment is approved prior to the nine-month deadline. Asking for an extension of the time to pay the tax may be part of the request for added time to file the return. Penalties apply to both late filing and payment. The penalty for failing to file on time is 5 percent of the amount of the tax due per month up to a maximum of 25 percent. Failure to pay the estate tax when due will incur penalties of ½ of 1 percent per month to a maximum of 25 percent.

Filing an estate tax return Form 706 is the mechanism for satisfying the IRS, even if no tax is due. According to the IRS, completing the various schedules and filing the return requires an estimated 21½ hours. Don't believe it! The IRS, in complying with the law requiring an estimate of time to file forms, fails to include the search time. Most of the time your executor will spend to complete Form 706 will be devoted to searching for and documenting information to be used in completing the schedules called for in Form 706. You can save your executor hours of time if you provide the information needed in a concise form, either by compiling the list of assets using the worksheets in Chapter 2 or by preparing a final letter that gives this information.

Complications in Gross Estate Calculation

Your executor's job of determining the value of assets in your estate is not straightforward. Generally, your gross estate includes everything you own as of the date of death. Few problems arise from that definition. But your gross estate may also include assets you did not own at death. Examples of such assets are:

• Outstanding dividends declared but not yet paid at time of death. (Dividends declared after death are clearly not included.)

• Unpaid interest that has accrued on certificates of deposit that are redeemable after death.

• U.S. Government bonds and other government agency debt instruments. These are included in your gross estate because the estate tax is a tax on the *transfer* of property, not on the property itself.

• Benefits paid under medical insurance if death resulted from an accident or similar occurrence that the policy covered. Medical policy reimbursements are includable if the decedent had a right to receive any funds at the time of death. A survivor's loss benefit from a similar policy is not includable in the decedent's estate.

• Income tax refund. Calculating the size of a tax refund can be difficult, but it must be considered as part of the gross estate.

• **Dower** and **curtesy interests** in a survivor's property. A dower interest is the part of a deceased husband's real property that goes to his widow for her lifetime. A curtesy interest is the part of a deceased wife's real property allowed to her husband on her death. These are legal entitlements; a will cannot cut a spouse out of his or her legal right to some portion of the decedent's property.

Often the IRS disagrees with values submitted in the various schedules that are a part of Form 706, such as Schedule A—Real Estate, for example. The law provides penalties for deliberate understatement of values. As recently as 1989 the Congress gave the IRS additional clout in dealing with attempts to foil the collection of estate taxes through undervaluations. First, an understatement may be penalized if the value of the property is stated at 25 percent less than the amount determined to be correct; the penalty is 40 percent of the underpayment attributable to a gross valuation misstatement. These new rules are effective for estate tax returns filed after December 31, 1989. For substantial estates the executor or trustee may withhold distributions until the IRS has examined and approved valuations stated in the return. Negotiating compromise valuations can drag out the settlement of an estate for months, possibly years.

Two Problem Areas

To avoid problems of valuation when filing estate tax returns, your executor should document figures wherever the chance of a disagreement occurs. Two prime areas for disagreement are real estate and closely held business interests.

Real Estate The IRS expects the executor to value real estate at its fair market value as of the date of death or six months later—executor's choice. Fair market value is the price at which a property would change hands between a willing buyer and a willing seller, when neither is forced to buy or to sell and when both have reasonable knowledge of all relevant facts. Fair market value may not be determined by a forced sale. The location of the property must be taken into account wherever appropriate. Expenses incurred in selling will be deducted to reach the fair market value. That said, the fair market value of real estate will most likely be determined by appraisal, possibly a consensus of appraisals. An expert appraiser will study the property and prepare a statement of value after citing conditions and his analysis to back up the valuation. A licensed appraiser's report will in most cases be acceptable in an IRS audit. An off-hand guess by a real estate salesperson could be challenged.

An executor should ask for an appraisal of any real estate among the assets as soon as possible, as market conditions may change rapidly and could affect an appraiser's thinking. At the same time an appraiser may suggest waiting to use the date six months after death if the real estate market appears to be declining. A lower appraisal later could affect taxes due on the total estate. If the real estate involves a farm, different rules may apply due to the huge appreciation that has boosted the value of farm land. These rules aim to protect the family's interest in continuing to farm the land and avoid having to sell it to pay estate taxes.

Closely Held Business or Business Interests A closely held business is one owned by a family or a few stockholders and shares are available to the public. Arriving at a fair market value for shares of a closely held business is difficult because the shares do not trade. Valuing the price of publicly traded issues at the market close on the day of death or a previous day if the markets are not open is simple; consult the tables of stock prices published in *The Wall Street Journal* or a large metropolitan newspaper. Closing prices represent a summary of decisions between buyers and sellers on an exchange.

Share prices of a private business or a closely held corporation are based on accounts, assets, earnings, and growth both past and potential. Comparisons with similar businesses whose shares are traded regularly may help if similar businesses exist and their accounts are accessible. If you are a minority stockholder and your executor attempted to sell shares in a closely held business, the share prices might not represent a proportional interest in the corporation. The IRS will accept a lower valuation because a minority owner has few privileges and exerts little control. Your executor should be advised to seek expert consultation in the evaluation of your shares in a small business whose shares do not trade.

Date of Valuation

If your executor elects to use the alternate date for valuing your real estate, he or she must value all of your estate on the alternate date—six months following your death. The alternate date may be used if it results in a lower tax. Thus, your executor may face the double duty—and your estate, the extra costs—of compiling an estate tax return for two different dates if there is a question of which date would lead to the lesser tax. If the executor elects the alternate date, six months after the decedent's death, any property distributed, sold, traded, or otherwise disposed of prior to the alternate date must be valued as of the date any of these actions occurred.

Filing Form 706

Instructions for filing Form 706, the estate tax return, include many details for valuing bonds, stocks, and other property. Numerous exceptions apply when using the alternate date of death, and it is these niceties of timing and determination that can require hours on the part of the executor to comply with government regulations.

If your taxable estate appears likely to exceed the $600,000 exemption, your executor should consult an accountant and possibly an attorney for help in filing the estate tax return. The 36 pages of Form 706 contain numerous schedules, all of which must be completed unless your executor can note a zero on the schedule. Form 706 aims to reach a figure that represents the true gross value of your estate as of the date of death or the alternate date six months later. Expenses, taxes, and fees may reduce that figure to less than $600,000. The more complicated your estate, the more schedules will apply and the more time and effort will be expended in completing the estate tax return.

Anticipation of possible federal estate taxes after your death can be the key to effective control of those estate taxes. If you complete the worksheets on pages 000-000 and find your taxable estate will exceed the exemption limit for estate taxes, you can take preventive action. Later on we will look

at different strategies for reducing the size of your estate to bring it into the tax-exempt category, such as gifts to heirs or charities. Right now, let's look at another way of minimizing taxes—the tax-saving trust.

Tax-Saving Trust

Using the tax-saving or bypass trust can save a couple many thousands of dollars in estate taxes. The tax-saving trust works equally well with a will or living trust. If you are using a will to convey property after your death, the tax-saving trust is written into the will and becomes effective during probate. Such trusts are called testamentary trusts. Similar tax-saving trusts may be known as A-B or A-B-C trusts in a living trust.

A tax-saving trust works like this: One half of a spouse's taxable property totalling no more than $60,000 of value is placed in trust while a husband and wife are living. A surviving spouse does not receive title to the property placed in the trust. Instead, the property is held in trust with income available to the surviving spouse during his or her lifetime. (Some invasion of the trust principal may be permitted under certain conditions.) The trust is managed by a trustee, who could be the surviving spouse. Assets are distributed to designated heirs after the surviving spouse dies. If the decedent's half of the couple's taxable estate exceeds the $600,000 exemption limit, the executor may decide to pay the estate tax after the first death. He or she may decide, however, to simply transfer all of the property above $600,000 to the surviving spouse. Estate taxes would then be paid following the second death. A surviving spouse could choose to give his or her family members or charities the money that would otherwise have gone for taxes. Another choice could be to make sure the surviving spouse has enough income from the assets to support his or her lifestyle and to provide medical care without running out of money.

Placing half of a couple's estate or up to $600,000 in the tax-saving trust uses the $192,800 exemption and no tax is due at the first death. Those assets, up to the $600,000 limit, are no longer a part of the surviving spouse's estate. At the second death only the surviving spouse's property is subject to estate taxes. See the box below for an example of the tax savings available from using the bypass trust.

Using a tax-saving trust depends on being able to divide a couple's property following the first death. In a community property state, which considers assets acquired by a married couple to be owned equally by the marriage partners, the division is provided by state law. In other states the **marital deduction** will normally be available. The marital deduction is equal to about half of an estate awarded to the surviving spouse upon the death of a marriage partner. However, the tax court recently denied the marital deduction to estates where the spouse is not a U.S. citizen.

BENEFITS OF A TAX-SAVING TRUST

Case No. 1—John Doe leaves everything to his wife, Jane, in a will

Taxable estate—$1,200,000—All to Jane Doe
No tax due at John Doe's death

At Jane Doe's death—

Total estate valuation	$1,200,000
Jane Doe's equivalent exemption	**(600,000)**
Taxable estate	$600,000
Tax on $500,000	$155,800
Tax on $100,000	**37,000**
Total federal tax	$192,800

Case No. 2—John Doe leaves tax-saving trust plus remainder to Jane Doe

Taxable estate—	$1,200,000
John's half of estate left in trust for Jane and later to children—Exemption	**$600,000**
Marital deduction of community property to Jane	$600,000
At Jane Doe's death—	
Taxable estate	$600,000
Equivalent exemption	**(600,000)**
Federal income tax due	0

Should You Pay Now or Later?

Tax planners generally advise putting off taxes as long as possible through legal means such as a bypass trust. As we have seen, for instance, the executor may pay some tax on the estate of the first person of a couple to die or postpone all taxes until after the second death. When a couple's taxable estates exceed $1.2 million, some estate or gift tax will be due eventually. Sometimes paying sooner may reduce the tax. For instance, paying tax on the excess over $600,000 after the first death and the tax on the excess after the second death will likely reduce the total estate tax liability, as shown in the example in the box on page 53 . But the future is not always crystal clear, and unforeseen events may reduce taxes even further. Not paying taxes after the first death leaves more assets available to the surviving spouse. He or she may spend more as inflation continues, or elect to give away enough assets to reduce the taxable estate value to $600,000 or less. Annual gifts of $10,000 may be given to family with no effect on estate or gift taxes. Practically unlimited amounts may be given to charities to reduce assets below taxable levels. A $10,000 gift to a favorite charity actually costs only $6,300 because it would avoid paying $3,700 in estate taxes at the margin. Another possibility is that earnings from assets over the limit at the first death could exceed the tax if they have several years to compound.

Paying Taxes

Paying estate taxes may be a burden, but the IRS insists on full payment with the filing of the estate tax return except in two cases:

• The executor may request an extension of time for paying the tax by filing four copies of Form 4768, as noted earlier. However, the tax is still due at the time of the filing for an extension unless the executor can show reasonable cause. A delay of up to 12 months may be allowed, but reasonable cause can be difficult to establish and requires approval before the estate tax return filing due date.

• Installment payments of the estate tax are permitted when a part of the decedent's assets includes an interest in a closely held business and the decedent was a U.S. citizen or resident at the time of death. Installment payments are limited to that portion of the decedent's assets related to the interest in the closely held business. For example, if 50 percent of the taxable estate is attributable to the closely held business, the executor would be limited to installment payments for 50 percent of the estate tax.

No other exceptions apply, even if the estate's assets do not include enough cash to pay the tax. The IRS requires an executor to convert assets to cash in order to pay the tax, even if a short term sale would bring less than optimum value.

State Estate or Inheritance Taxes

Laws for taxing estates at the state level are a hodgepodge of different and conflicting statutes, exemption levels and rates. Table 3B indicates the status of state taxes on estates and/or inheritances. Estate taxes are levied on the taxable estate of the decedent. State laws change frequently. Check your state's estate tax code to be sure you understand the latest rules and rates. Inheritance taxes are levied on taxable amounts received by an heir. Exemptions may eliminate taxes on inheritances in some states depending on the relationship, if any, between the heir and the decedent.

ALTERNATIVE TAXES—ESTATE OVER $1,200,000

Case No. 1—John and Jane Doe's taxable estate valued at $1,600,000

At John's death—Estate	$1,600,000
Tax-saving trust for exemption	(600,000)
All of excess over $600,000 to Jane	**$1,000,000**
No tax due	
At Jane' death—Estate	$1,000,000
Jane's equivalent exemption	**(600,000)**
Taxable remainder	$400,000
Tax —$150,000 at 37%	55,500
—$250,000 at 39%	**97,500**
Total tax	$153,000

Case No. 2—John and Jane Doe's taxable estate valued at $1,600,000

At John's death—Estate	$1,600,000
Divided equally	**800,000**
John's half	$800,000
Tax-saving trust for exemption	**(600,000)**
Taxable remainder	$200,000
Tax—$150,000 at 37%	55,500
—$50,000 at 39%	**19,500**
Total tax due	$75,000
At Jane's death—Estate	$800,000
Equivalent exemption	**(600,000)**
Taxable remainder	$200,000
Tax—$150,000 at 37%	55,500
—$50,000 at 39%	**19,500**
Total tax due	$75,000
Net saving—$3,000	

TABLE 3B—State Inheritance or Estate Taxes

State	Inheritance Taxes	Estate Taxes	State	Inheritance Taxes	Estate Taxes
Alabama	No	PU	Montana	Yes	No
Alaska	No	PU	Nebraska	Yes	No
Arizona	No	PU	Nevada	No	No
Arkansas	No	Pu	New Hampshire	Yes	No
California	No	PU	New Jersey	Yes	No
Colorado	No	PU	New Mexico	No	PU
Connecticut	Yes	No	New York	No	Yes
Delaware	Yes	No	North Carolina	Yes	No
District of Columbia	No	PU	North Dakota	No	PU
Florida	No	PU	Ohio	No	Yes·
Georgia	No	PU	Oklahoma	Yes	No
Hawaii	No	PU	Oregon	No	PU
Idaho	Yes	No	Pennsylvania	Yes	No
Illinois	No	PU	Rhode Island	No	Yes
Indiana	Yes	No	South Carolina	No	Yes
Iowa	Yes	No	South Dakota	Yes	No
Kansas	Yes	No	Tennessee	Yes	No
Kentucky	Yes	No	Texas	No	PU
Louisiana	Yes	No	Utah	No	PU
Maine	No	PU	Vermont	No	PU
Maryland	Yes	No	Virginia	No	PU
Massachusetts	No	Yes	West Virginia	No	PU
Michigan	Yes	No	Washington	No	PU
Minnesota	No	PU	Wisconsin	Yes	No
Mississippi	No	Yes	Wyoming	No	PU
Missouri	No	PU			

PU—Pick up tax if a federal estate tax is payable

As you can see in Table 3B, some states levy what is commonly known as a **pickup tax**, a relatively minor tax. It is equal to the maximum credit for state taxes allowed on a federal estate tax return. Table 3C sets out the progressive rates for a typical state estate or inheritance credit to be applied against a federal estate tax. Note the "Adjusted Taxable Estate." This is the amount left from the taxable estate after deducting $60,000. Suppose your taxable estate totals $700,000. Deducting $60,000 leaves an adjusted taxable estate of $640,000. Your state tax credit would be $18,000 with additional amounts taxed at 4.8 percent up to the next bracket of $840,000 (adjusted).

Since the credit of $18,000 is allowed dollar for dollar against the federal estate tax liability, those states where the pickup tax is noted in Table 3B collect that amount. Your estate would pay no additional taxes overall. The $18,000 would be paid to the state and an equal amount would be taken as a credit against the federal estate tax due. Residents of those states where a pickup tax applies pay no effective state estate tax.

Other states may collect an estate tax or an inheritance tax. The pickup tax is then based on the level of a decedent's estate for federal tax purposes. If no federal estate tax is due, then no state pickup tax is due.

No state currently collects both an estate and an inheritance tax, although in the past several states have collected both. Nevada is the only state that collects no pickup tax, estate tax, or inheritance tax.

TABLE 3C—State Death Tax Credit Rate Schedule

Adjusted Taxable Estate*		Maximum Tax Credit	
Over	But not over	Of the excess over	
$0	$90,000	$0 + 0.8%	$40,000
$90,000	$140,000	$400 + 1.6%	$90,000
$140,000	$240,000	$1,200 + 2.4%	$140,000
$240,000	$440,000	$3,600 + 3.2%	$240,000
$440,000	$640,000	$10,000 + 4%	$440,000
$640,000	$840,000	$18,000 + 4.8%	$640,000
$840,000	$1,040,000	$27,600 + 5.6%	$840,000
$1,040,000	$1,540,000	$38,800 + 6.4%	$1,040,000
$1,540,000	$2,040,000	$70,800 + 7.2%	$1,540,000
$2,040,000	$2,540,000	$106,800 + 8%	$2,040,000
$2,540,000	$3,040,000	$146,800 + 8.8%	$2,540,000
$3,040,000	$3,540,000	$190,800 + 9.6%	$3,040,000
$3,540,000	$4,040,000	$238,800 + 10.4%	$3,540,000
$4,040,000	$5,040,000	$290,800 + 11.2%	$4,040,000
$5,040,000	$6,040,000	$402,800 + 12%	$5,040,000
$6,040,000	$7,040,000	$522,800 + 12.8%	$6,040,000
$7,040,000	$8,040,000	$650,800 + 13.6%	$7,040,000
$8,040,000	$9,040,000	$786,800 +14.4%	$8,040,000
$9,040,000	$10,040,000	$930,800 + 15.2%	$9,040,000
$10,040,000	—	$1,082,800 + 16%	$10,040,000

*Taxable estate reduced by $60,000

In those states that collect either an estate or inheritance tax, exemptions, rates, and rules range all over the place. An estate will be taxed on a progressive schedule at lower rates than the federal unified gift and estate tax schedule. Those states with estate or inheritance taxes will normally tax gifts as well, similar to the gift tax schedules at the federal level. As of June 30, 1990, 20 states had taxes on inheritances, and 6 states had taxes on estates. The number of states taxing estates or inheritances appears to be declining. States have repealed statutes for these taxes, often referred to as "death taxes," under pressure from voters or as a result of successful initiatives.

Classes of Heirs

One of the common schedules for state inheritance taxes charges heirs different rates according to their relationship to the decedent. A surviving spouse and direct lineal descendants may be totally exempt from taxes. Brothers, sisters, sons- or daughters-in-law, and in-laws of descendants would gain some exemption and pay a tax on amounts over the exemption level. More distant relatives and others may be entitled to a minimal or no exemption and pay a higher rate on amounts over the exemption. Typically, there are three classes of heirs, referred to as Class A, B, or C. If a state divides relationships into four classes, they will usually be numbered 1 through 4. Class differences do not affect state estate taxes because they are paid by the estate before distribution of assets, although Wisconsin denotes four classes as A through D.

Table 3D is a model state inheritance tax schedule drawn to illustrate several typical provisions. Note that the surviving spouse and children are exempt from all taxes on inheritances. Progression brackets are the same for all four classes, but tax rates increase as heirs are more distant from the decedent.

One interesting ploy to reduce inheritance taxes substantially is what's known as **adult adoption**. Normally, one thinks of adoption in terms of babies or young children. However, in some but not all of the 20 states currently taxing inheritances, adult adoption is permitted. When a person who would ordinarily receive an inheritance as a Class C heir moves up to Class A through adoption, all or a large part of the inheritance tax goes away. Some legal work is necessary to petition a court for adoption, but the cost of these documents is minimal compared to the savings in state inheritance taxes. Obviously each case must be considered on its own merits, as only a few states continue to permit adult adoptions. The following example illustrates how adult adoption reduces an inheritance tax. This case is taken from the book *Adopt Your Way to Inheritance and Gift Tax Savings*, by Charles P. Moriarty, Jr. (Writing Works, 1980).

Henry J. was a widower getting along in years. His estate had escalated to more than $1,100,000. He had named his cousin, Nancy, and her two children as his heirs. Nancy was a widow and had been doing okay financially, but there was no money to send the two kids to college. Under the state's inheritance tax schedules, a $1 million estate left to Nancy would be taxed at $241,500 because she and the children were Class C heirs. If they were Class A heirs, the inheritance tax would drop to $86,500 for a difference of $155,000.

Henry's attorney suggested an adoption, but Henry objected immediately. "Wouldn't

TABLE 3D

State Inheritance Tax Schedule
(Varies by State)

Typical

Class 1: Spouse, lineal descendants and ancestors
Class 2: Siblings, children of siblings, daughter- or son-in-law
Class 3: Uncles, aunts and first cousins
Class 4: All others

Inheritance Tax Schedule

Taxable Inheritance	Tax Rate Class 1	Class 2	Class 3	Class 4
$0 – $25,000	2%	4%	6%	8%
$25,000 – $50,000	4%	8%	12%	16%
$50,000 – $100,000	6%	12%	18%	24%
Over $100,000	8%	16%	24%	32%

Exemptions: 1. Spouse or child—All inheritances exempt
2. Lineal ancestors—$9,000 exempt
3. Class 2—$1,000
4. Classes 3 & 4—No exemption

adopting the two children cut them off from their natural family relations?" he asked.

"Yes, but I was thinking of Nancy," the attorney replied. "If you adopt Nancy, then the children are descendants of an adopted person and all three move up to become Class A heirs. The children retain their usual family rights."

Domicile

Where you live can affect how much you pay in state taxes. If you own property in different states or have lived in different places during your lifetime, you could end up paying taxes in two or more states. Part of your estate planning should be directed to establishing your legal home or **domicile.** Just as they have different rules and tax schedules that apply to state estate or inheritance taxes, various states define domicile differently. Or, tax collectors may interpret various factors in favor of the state.

If you are living in a state and die there, that state will claim you as a resident. "Living" in a location may be defined as including being a resident most of the year, voting as a resident, paying taxes on property you own in the state, attending and contributing to a church, belonging to one or more organizations in the state, registering one or more cars in the state, and being paid by an employer while working at an office or plant in the state. Not all of these requirements are needed to establish a domicile, but a state tax authority might assert any or all of these state residency requirements.

Your own intentions can be important. You may assert your intentions of becoming a citizen of a state by saying so and doing any or all of the things noted earlier. Problems may arise if you lived in another state previous to the one you are now living in. One indication that you may not have given up your domicile in another state is your ownership of a house there. Mobile Americans move on average about once every five years. If you continue to own a house in State A after moving to State B, State A will probably attempt to collect state estate taxes if the state's laws require a tax. Or if part of your family, say your parents or a brother, continue to live in State A after you have moved to State B or possibly even to State C or D, State A might try to claim you are domiciled in State A—and attempt to collect state estate or inheritance taxes.

Owning property in more than one state continues to cause problems with multiple taxes on a decedent's estate. Even if you own a recreational cabin on some remote lake, a state could claim estate or inheritance taxes. A common problem involves the retiree who lives in two states, one in the sunbelt during the winter and one up north in the summer. Which state is he domiciled in? Both, according to state tax authorities. A change in ownership through probate or a trust tips off authorities that a death has occurred. And this tip starts up the collection process.

Property other than real estate, such as stocks and bonds, may actually be taxed two or more times by different states. Obviously, this personal property is not tied to a specific state location. But, if a state prevails in court to establish a decedent's domicile in State A and another court establishes the decedent's domicile in State B, the estate could pay double taxes. The fact that State A has taxed the stocks and bonds does not deter State B from asserting its own claim. Unfortunately, the United States Supreme Court has upheld states' rights in asserting multiple claims against an estate. Claims may have any number of bases, including insurance policies, state income tax returns filed as a resident rather than a nonresident, maintenance of church membership in two or more congregations, and keeping a safe deposit box in the state.

Establishing one's domicile is a matter of severing all connections with all states other than the one you are now living in. Change your voting registration, formally resign membership in a church, clubs, and organizations before taking on new memberships at your new location. Instead of owning houses in two states, pick the one where you prefer to live and sell the other. If you wish to "visit" your previous home, even for several months each year, rent a house. Switch doctors, dentists, and health plans to your preferred domicile. Of course, you will want to investigate the estate and inheritance taxes in a new state. Some persons consider the state tax environment a key factor in deciding where to retire. None of the sunbelt states exact an estate tax other than the pickup tax. Among the states along the southern tier of the United States, only Louisiana has an inheritance tax.

If your estate is likely to be substantial, consult with an attorney about the steps you should take to establish a definite domicile in only one state, preferably a state without an estate or inheritance tax.

Conclusion

Planning your estate effectively depends on knowing the potential taxes that may be levied to reduce the assets you expect to pass along to your spouse, children, and others.

Federal estate and gift taxes are the most pervasive, as they apply to everyone. However, state estate or inheritance taxes may also prove to be a burden unless you plan to minimize their impact. Mainly, you should be aware of the possibility of multiple state taxes as two or more states may claim taxes based on different conditions that define your domicile.

CHAPTER FOUR

Will and Probate

KEY TERMS IN THIS CHAPTER

succession	*contingencies*
titled property	*witnesses*
holographic will	*probate estate*
oral will	*testate*
codicil	*interested person*
pour-over will	*letters testamentary*

Wills have long been the legal way to transfer property between generations. But, over the past few decades wills and probate have garnered reams of unfavorable publicity, much of it justified. High costs and long delays with little feeling for the heirs are among the primary complaints. Yet, probate courts continue to oversee most of the business of settling estates and distributing decedents' property. The probate court functions in every community and gets involved in one of two ways:

• A will drawn up by a decedent, usually with the aid and advice of an attorney, is presented for probate. The word probate comes from the root meaning "to prove." A valid will is a document whose contents are legally enforceable, and it is the task of probate court to prove that the will is valid.

• A decedent dies without leaving a valid will. State statutes control the distribution of a person's property unless there is a valid will to override the state's "law of **succession**." In such a case, the probate court oversees the distribution of property according to the state's law.

So—you have a choice. You may allow your property to be distributed according to state statutes. Or, you may develop your own will that will allow your executor to distribute your assets to the persons or organizations you choose. Many people have so little property, there is little or no need for probate. The valuation of rates that must pass through probate ranges from $2,000 to $100,000 in different states. Whatever the limit, **titled property** (house or car, for example) will almost always have to pass through probate for the title change to be legal. If titled property is owned jointly with right of survivorship, then the survivor owns the property. But, when the survivor dies, a title change at that point will require probate court action.

The probate court does more than prove wills and distribute property. It oversees paying the bills a decedent leaves behind. Probate is the only legal process for transferring the title to real estate and other titled property (cars, boats, etc.) if you, as the owner, should become incapacitated and unable to sign your name. If a minor inherits titled property, the probate court must approve a sale of that property.

Drafting Your Will

"Can I write out my own will in my own handwriting and make it legal?" A **holographic will**, that is, one that is handwritten, will be recognized in half of the states. It must be dated and signed, but does not need to be witnessed in many states. In New York, a holographic will must be witnessed except for those of individuals in the armed forces. While you may get away with writing your will in this way, don't count on it. Probate courts may consider it a forgery, and there are no witnesses around to vouch for it.

Oral wills, sometimes made when a person is on the brink of death, may be acceptable, but use one only in an emergency. California, for example, only accepts an oral will if the maker is in military service just before death. The amount that can be transferred is limited to $1,000. Despite the march of technology, video or film wills are not acceptable in any of the 50 states.

You're better off to ask for legal help to prepare even the simplest of wills and follow the rules for witnessing it. When you are ready to draft a last will and testament for yourself alone or with your spouse, consult an attorney—one experienced in drafting wills. Tax and probate law is a specialty; you should hire an attorney who practices that specialty.

We have already seen the important reasons for drafting a will. Once drafted, however, a will may need to be updated. Here are three reasons why a will may need revision:

1. The law of estates and federal taxes has changed enough since 1988 to warrant an update. The major change was the opportunity for one spouse to leave all assets to the surviving spouse. If you have a will that is more than two years old, you should at least have it reviewed. Depending on how your existing will is written, you may need a complete rewrite or only a **codicil** or two. A codicil is a formal amendment to a will that is prepared, signed, and witnessed.

2. Moving from a community property state to a common law state or vice versa can change the requirements for a will enough to warrant writing a new will. Various states may also handle state inheritance or estate taxes differently. If you have moved recently from one state to another, consult a knowledgeable attorney in your new state about your present will and how it fits the state's laws.

3. If you draft a will leaving substantial property to your spouse and then divorce, draft a new will based on an entirely new estate plan.

While the living trust is emerging as the method of choice for distributing property, there are good reasons to opt for a will over a living trust or for having both:

1. A will may transfer any property not included in a living trust. The **pour-over will**, for instance, "pours over" into the living trust any property not already transferred into it. Property acquired only a short time before death that might not have been transferred into a living trust is also handled by a will. A sudden acquisition may occur by gift or inheritance. In some cases a future inheritance destined for you may still be locked up in the probate of the will of the decedent. A pour-over will can handle these contingencies.

2. If your family includes minor children, only a will enables you to name a guardian if both you and your spouse should die. If you are a single parent, a will authorizes the person you name to care for your children until they reach their majority. A living trust cannot do this job for you. A living trust can be set up to provide funds to the guardian. A testamentary trust that goes into effect at the probate of a will can accomplish the same objective.

3. Although a living trust can simplify and expedite the distribution of your property, it may be more than you need if your estate is small. Depending on the state where you live, an informal or small estate proceeding may suffice. A simple will without complicated bequests could quickly and easily wind up your affairs.

4. While almost everyone who owns some property needs either a will or living trust to guide the distribution of that property, a young person or couple may find the living trust too complex for a long period. They could make a simple will now as a protection against disaster. Later, a living trust might be more appropriate.

There are, however, some things a will can't do. The following items are excluded from a will:

1. *Jointly owned property with right of survivorship*. If the joint owner survives the decedent, the survivor owns the property. When property is owned as tenants in common, which is joint ownership without right of survival, the decedent's interest can be willed to whomever he or she chooses. (See Chapter 7.)

2. *Property that has been moved into a living trust*. This property no longer belongs to the decedent, and thus, cannot be willed. The major reason for the living trust is to remove property from the decedent's probate estate.

3. *Death benefits from an insurance policy on the life of the decedent*. These go directly to the beneficiary or beneficiaries. The value of the death benefits are swept into the decedent's gross estate for tax purposes. If the beneficiary also owns the insurance policy on the decedent's life and the decedent has retained no incidents of ownership, such as the right to change a beneficiary or borrow against the cash value, the beneficiary receives the death benefits directly. The death benefits also escape being counted among the decedent's gross assets.

4. *Assets intended to provide retirement income, such as pension, profit sharing plans, 401(k), 403(b), Individual Retirement Account (IRA) and Keogh plans*. These assets go directly to named beneficiaries. They do not pass through the probate process but are counted in the gross estate.

5. *POD (pay on death) accounts, E-, EE-, H-, or HH-bonds and informal bank trust accounts*. These go directly to the beneficiary noted on the account or named on the savings bonds.

You may leave your property to almost anyone you choose, with a few limitations. In a community property state only half of the community property is yours to give away to anyone or any institution. In a common law state, spouses are entitled to some minimum of the couple's assets. You may not leave assets in a trust without some termination, even if that final day is years off. The IRS requires a trust to have some termination date or be dependent on some future happening, such as the death of a beneficiary. Nor may you reward anyone for doing a nonsocial deed, for instance, requiring a relative to divorce a spouse.

You may disinherit anyone except a spouse; he or she is entitled by law to some portion of your estate. You may disinherit a child or grandchild by avoiding any mention of the child in the will. However, a more practical method is to give the unfavored child $1 to establish your intent. A token bequest avoids the possible contest of a will with the assertion that you simply "forgot." Disinheriting a son or daughter, or grandchildren if a son or daughter has died, is serious business. Talk it over with your attorney, as your actions could lead to a legal contest of the will.

If you plan to leave property to minors, you should probably leave the assets in a Uniform Gifts to Minors Act or Uniform Transfer to Minors Act trust. (See Chapter 5.) Minors may not own more than a minimal amount of property in their own name and no property that requires their signature to effect a sale or transfer of title.

In drafting a will you should provide for various **contingencies**. One of the most common is what happens to the portion of your estate that you leave to your children if one of them should die before you? You need a decision tree that runs something like this: If a child is not married, your property is evenly divided among the re-

maining living children. If the child is married, his or her share goes to his widow or her widower and children if any. If both the child and spouse are killed in a common accident, the child's share is divided equally among his or her living children. If your child has done his or her job, the child will have written a will to name a guardian for minor children. A variety of contingencies need to be provided for, and a knowledgeable attorney will be versed in developing various lines of succession.

When you are satisfied with the provisions of your will, it must be signed and witnessed in a manner prescribed by your state's law. Typically, a will requires the signatures of two or three **witnesses**. You must meet with the witnesses in one place and sign the will in their presence. They sign to guarantee that your signature is truly yours.

Witnesses must meet several requirements: They must be adults, age 18 and older in most states. They will preferably be younger than you if there is a choice. Select witnesses who will be easy to locate at the time of your death. Remember, witnesses may be called into probate court as part of the "proving" process to authenticate your will. Another requirement is that a witness may not participate in any way in bequests from the estate.

Some people leave the original of a will with an attorney. A better way is to leave the signed and witnessed original of your will in your safe deposit box when state statutes do not require a court order to open it after the owner's death. A final letter prepared by you (see Chapter 12) will advise your surviving spouse or executor of the will's location. Make photocopies of the will to keep in your home file for reference.

Levels of Probate Actions

Depending on the state where you live, you will have access to one or more of the following three options regarding the probate process.

Informal or unsupervised probate may be used for handling small estates, particularly when no titled property is included in the probate estate. An informal probate may be specified in a will. Generally, agreement among the heirs to the informal process is a necessary first step. If one of the heirs objects to the will or the process, then the probate moves up to a formal or supervised action. Your executor may be able to handle simple, informal actions without the aid of an attorney, particularly when the probate estate is relatively small.

Some small estates that transfer very limited amounts of property require even less probate attention than the informal process. Jointly owned property, for instance, goes to the surviving owner and won't be part of the probate estate. Most of this process involves an affidavit that lists property and who is to receive it. Such affidavits can be approved by a court with minimum review.

Formal, supervised probate action results when the probate court supervises the entire proceedings. Supervised probates are required when probate estate assets exceed a limit, usually $60,000 but it varies by state, or when titled property is involved. Titled property is mainly real estate. Formal reports from appraisers, accountants, and attorneys will be reviewed by the court at each stage in the proceeding. With this level of supervision, time and costs escalate significantly. A supervised probate proceeding will almost always be required if one or more of the heirs contests the will, or there is a lack of agreement among the heirs.

The Truth About Probate

Considering that the probate process has been around for hundreds of years in various forms, a surprising volume of misinformation about it appears to be floating around. Here are some popular conceptions about probate and explanations of whether they're true or false.

Belief #1: A will avoids probate.
Fact: Definitely not so. A will facilitates the probate process, but wills and probate are inextricably woven together.

Belief #2: Probate can be expensive.
Fact: True. Normal costs range from about 5 to 15 percent of the gross estate. For relatively small estates in the range of $100,000, costs may mount to $10,000 to $20,000.

Belief #3: Probate is a lengthy routine procedure.
Fact: True. Probate cases typically run for a year to a year and a half. The time is almost completely unrelated to the size of the estate. Delays can be monumental if any part of the procedure is contested.

Belief #4: Everything one owns goes through probate.
Fact: False. Most property is included within the **probate estate**, that portion of one's gross estate that is involved in the probate process. But jointly owned property with right of survivorship goes directly

to the surviving joint owner. Life insurance benefits may go directly to the owner of the policy on the life of the decedent. If the decedent owns the policy, the proceeds are included in his or her probate estate. Assets transferred before death to a living trust escape probate, a key advantage of the living trust.

Belief #5: Everything in probate court is open to the public.

Fact: False. The estates of prominent people usually surface during probate. Since all court actions, including the presentation of facts and figures related to the estate, are conducted openly, nothing is private.

Steps in Probate

Proceedings vary by state and according to the value of the probate estate. An executor named in a will or an administrator appointed by a probate court can expect to proceed through these steps in a formal or supervised action:

First, if the decedent dies **testate**, that is, leaving a valid will, the appointed executor's first duty is to find the signed and witnessed original copy of the decedent's will. A thoughtful person will have noted the location of the will in his or her final papers or possibly in his or her last letter. If the executor is advised of his or her appointment by the decedent prior to his or her death, the executor should ask where the will is kept. A surviving spouse or close relative may know where to look for the will if it is not immediately apparent. Once the will has been located, the executor must determine whether it is the "last will and testament" or whether another will has superseded it, and whether it may have been amended by one or more codicils.

If the decedent died intestate, some "**interested person**," that is, someone affected by the estate, such as a creditor, heir, or relative, may file a written request for probate with the probate clerk in the county or city. The clerk will take action to get the case on the court's agenda. A first step is the appointment of an administrator to manage the probate process.

Second, an executor, who could be the surviving spouse, initiates the probate process by filing a request with the court clerk. This "petition for probate" is a simple form that gathers essential information, such as the name of the decedent and the names and addresses of relatives and likely heirs.

Third, the probate court judge approves the executor or personal representative (PR), if there is one; that is, if there is a will. If there is no will, the judge appoints a PR or administrator. The executor, PR, or administrator is the key person involved in managing the decedent's estate. This person is legally empowered to wind up affairs in an honest and efficient manner when the court issues "**letters testamentary**" or an equivalent. This document carries court authority and enables the executor to gain access to various accounts or documents needed for the probate. If the executor fails to act prudently, he could be held legally accountable by heirs who claim he failed to do his job effectively.

Fourth, once approved by the court, the executor must notify interested persons of the probate proceeding. To assure no one is omitted, the executor should publish a notice in a newspaper that circulates in the decedent's community. He will also send registered letters to interested persons. These notices include a deadline for the filing of claims by interested persons. The costs of these notices, including newspaper advertisements, are paid by the estate. A waiting period follows the notices, so that creditors and others may file claims before the deadline.

Fifth, getting down to the nitty-gritty, the executor assembles an inventory of the decedent's estate. How much of this work was done by the decedent in preparing an estate plan affects the time and workload of the executor. The end product will be a complete listing of the decedent's assets and their value; real and personal property of substantial value will have been appraised. In collecting this information the executor will need to use the letters testamentary from the probate court. Otherwise, bank and thrift officers are not authorized to divulge information they have regarding the decedent's assets.

Valuing a decedent's personal property requires judgment. Not every sock or undergarment needs to be listed and appraised for its fair market value. However, antiques, keepsakes, jewelry, knick-knacks, and similar goods may need to be listed with a dollar value attached. Any property owned jointly with a surviving spouse can be set aside to minimize the size of the probate estate. Some states set probate fees as a percentage of the probate estate; so, the smaller the probate estate, the lower the costs of the probate proceedings. In many cases the executor or PR can accomplish much of the detail work and minimize the costs of accountants and appraisers.

Sixth, paying legitimate creditor claims begins the unwinding process. The executor is required to examine creditor claims for accuracy and legitimacy. Some bills may have already been paid. Or, goods that were never delivered may be billed. Debts paid reduce the gross estate and avoid possible taxation.

Taxes are the executor's next job. Court fees, attorney's fees, and other costs must be accounted for, and they can be substantial. Some states set the fee schedules for the court and attorney regardless of the amount of work involved. Often attorneys bill for additional services over the statutory amount permitted. The executor should ask the probate court for help to determine when specific fees are due and how they might be calculated. Executors, personal representatives, and administrators are entitled to fees for their work in winding up an estate. Usually, the fee schedules are related to the size of the estate.

Seventh, the executor prepares a final accounting of debts, costs, and valuation, usually with the help of an accountant. The final accounting looks much like a balance sheet that sets off assets and liabilities. Debts, taxes, outstanding liabilities plus any sources of income, such as interest on accounts, will be clearly spelled out. Before it is accepted, the executor will send copies of the final accounting to the court and to interested parties for review. Heirs may challenge the accounting if it doesn't seem favorable to their claims.

Eighth, finally, and usually to the utter dismay of the heirs, the executor or personal representative distributes the decedent's property in accordance with provisions of the will. However, if the probate results from intestacy, the court's administrator will follow the state's statutes on succession.

Ninth, a final act by the executor or administrator in closing the file is to submit a statement under oath that the business of the estate is finished. A formal hearing on the matter may be held in the probate court to offer a final forum for complaints, if any.

Conclusion

Using a will and the probate system is the common way to resolve the affairs of the decedent. A will and probate may not be the most efficient or effective system. Some estates can be better served with a living trust. Other estates with unique requirements, such as the need to name a personal guardian for minor children, may use only a will or a will plus a living trust.

Understanding how a will and probate court function is an integral part of estate planning. Use the information as a tool for evaluating your alternatives.

CHAPTER FIVE

Living Trust

KEY TERMS IN THIS CHAPTER

inter vivos	trust estate
creator	trust agreement
grantor	pay-on-death
donor	CUSIP
settlor	Uniform Gifts (or Transfers) to
trustor	Minors Act
trustee	custodian
beneficiary	correction deed

A living trust is a useful alternative to a will for conveying your property to heirs and others. The living trust may also be known as **inter vivos** trust—for *among the living*, meaning one that is created while you are living. A living trust affords two big advantages over a will:

• Delays are minimal. Money and other property can be immediately transferred to those persons and/or institutions named in the trust.

• Setting up, maintaining and settling a living trust will usually cost only a fraction of the expenses of writing and probating a will.

Despite these and other advantages of a living trust, only about 1 to 2 percent of people who develop an estate plan elect to use one. The number is rising as more people learn about it.

A living trust is a legal entity that "owns" all or most of your property. The living trust differs from the testamentary trust of a will in that it must be started during your lifetime. The testamentary trust begins only at death, after probate. The living trust is revocable during your lifetime, that is, it may be changed as often as you wish or rewritten entirely while you are alive. All or that portion of the living trust that covers your estate becomes irrevocable at your death.

Don't confuse the term living will with the living trust. A living will documents your wishes about continuing heroic measures to maintain life in case you become incompetent; it does nothing to distribute your estate at death.

States can create two types of entities: corporations and trusts. In many ways corporations and trusts function as if they were real persons. They may appear at times to have lives of their own. Trusts operate with far more restrictions than corporations, but they can still be extremely useful. A living trust can do the following:

• Protect information regarding the size and form of your property from the prying eyes of the public and possible heirs because it is not open to public scrutiny.

• Afford an efficient route to distributing your property at death. Financial planners, bank officers, stock brokers, some attorneys, and others flatly state that the living trust is the only practical method for conveying one's property to others following death.

• Provide assets for your support and management in case you become incompetent. Thus, a living trust provides for your compassionate care while living and for the orderly distribution of your assets at death.

Origin of Trusts

Trusts first appeared in Roman times as a means for distributing one's assets to someone other than the eldest son who was otherwise the sole inheritor. Emperor Augustus (63 B.C.–14 A.D.) is credited with easing the lack of generosity relatives often suffered at the hands of the eldest son; many were almost totally disenfranchised. From those early times, the trust developed as a means of guiding the person receiving property according to instructions handed down by the grantor, the person who left property to others at his death. Then, for 12 centuries the concept of the trust disappeared. It reappeared in thirteenth-century England to correct three problems with the civil law of the time: property could not be willed to someone, only the eldest son could

inherit a father's estate, and a bride's personal property became the bridegroom's absolute property at marriage.

But, numerous problems continued to plague England's women and younger sons. A friend may have been asked or commanded to manage a person's property during that person's lifetime. At death the "friend" would take charge of land and other property, turning rents and income over to a widow or others. This system worked well as long as the "friend" was a trustworthy fellow. Betrayals by friends became so frequent, however, that in the fourteenth century a chancery court took over the control for the benefit of a decedent's widow and children. When the word got around that a chancellor could and would enforce the instructions of a decedent to a friend, the plan became increasingly popular. From these modest beginnings the modern trust concept developed to settle the distribution of family property. The success of these early trusts was highly dependent on the level of confidence and capability enjoyed by the friend or settlor empowered to manage the property.

Since much of the law in the United States came over with early immigrants from England, the concept of trusts as used in the United States emerged from these early beginnings. A living trust is only one of many trusts that have been found useful for a variety of purposes. (See Chapter 6 for more on different types of trusts.)

Definitions

Five basic terms are important for understanding trusts:

• The **creator**, also known as the **grantor, donor, settlor,** or **trustor,** is the person who establishes or sets up the trust.

• The **trustee** is the person or institution entrusted to carry out the terms of the trust; that is, the person who turns property owned by one person over to another in accordance with the written instructions of the creator. A trustee may be a relative, friend, lawyer, a bank, trust company, or other institution. A surviving or successor trustee is one who continues to manage assets in the trust should the primary trustee(s) die or become incompetent. A well-drawn living trust should name one or more successor trustees to assure continued management. A successor trustee may not be as closely related to the creator or trustor as the primary trustee or have the same interest. However, a successor trustee must function with fiduciary responsibility; that is, prudently and strictly in accordance with the trust agreement.

• A **beneficiary** is a person who receives property from the creator according to provisions of the living trust. Many beneficiaries with varied rights may be provided for in the trust.

• The **trust estate** includes all of the property legally transferred to the trust by the creator for the benefit of the beneficiaries. The trust estate may also be called the trust fund if most of the property is cash or securities. However, the trust estate may include all manner of assets and property.

• The **trust agreement** is the legal document that sets forth the terms of the trust and how it is to be administered.

Advantages of a Living Trust

The primary advantage of a living trust is that of avoiding probate. Sometimes the living trust is called a "probate avoidance trust." If the procedures and costs of a will and probate were less onerous, there would be little need for a living trust as a means of avoiding probate. Additional advantages of the living trust include the following.

Control

You maintain complete control over your property during your lifetime. If you should become incompetent; that is, unable to function either mentally, physically, or both, a successor trustee is empowered to act for you. You may elect to engage a trustee to handle your assets, so you can monitor his or her progress. If you are not happy with the trustee's style of management or the results, you can fire him and hire another. If you choose a trustee who acts only after your death, you may have no idea of his or her ability. In most states, you are the trustee of your own living trust while you are living and remain competent. A few states do not permit the creator of a trust to be its trustee.

Avoiding Delays

Delays often complicate dispersal of assets through the lengthy process of probating a will. With a living trust, your assets are owned by the trust and managed by a trustee. At your death the trustee simply changes the title to the property that is in the trust to the person designated. For example, the trust owns shares of XYZ Corp. When the creator of the trust dies, stock certificates are forwarded to the transfer agent who reissues the stock to the beneficiary named in the trust, using the trust agreement and a death certificate as authority. No court is involved. The trust can be terminated as soon as the trustee satisfies the IRS that all of its provisions have been met.

Maintaining Privacy

A trust agreement is a document drawn by an attorney in consultation with the creator, the trustee, and possibly some of the beneficiaries. None of its provisions are open to the public, and nothing appears in an open courtroom. This feature is in direct contrast to the public disclosure afforded by a will and its provisions.

Lower Costs

Two costs are involved in a living trust. First, an attorney prepares the trust agreement. It will include a number of "boilerplate" clauses that are a part of every agreement. But the key parts of the trust agreement are unique and must be tailored to suit your requirements. Although you can put together a trust agreement yourself from so-called standard forms, you should avoid this route. The cost of not availing yourself of the experience of an attorney— through errors or omissions—could be greater than a lawyer's fee. Typically, the cost of preparing the trust agreement runs from $1,000 to $3,000, depending on its complexity and contingencies.

Second, fees paid to the trustee for managing the trust continue during your lifetime and after death until all property is distributed. You avoid this fee if you or your spouse acts as the trustee, and this is the case with most living trusts where permitted. If you manage your own living trust, you save the fee. A relative may act for you as trustee after death, also without taking a fee, to minimize this expense. If a bank or other institution performs the trustee's functions, expect to pay a fee that may range from ¾ of 1 percent to 1 percent of the trust assets per year with numerous additional fees for special services. Combined, these fees will likely be far lower than comparable expenses for probate unless the living trust continues for a number of years under the direction of a paid trustee. (See Table 5A for a comparison of the costs of wills and living trusts.)

TABLE 5A—Comparative Costs of Will versus Living Trust

Estate Valued at $500,000*

Will

Original drafting of will	$400.00
Probate costs @ 9 percent**	4,500.00
	$4,900.00

Living Trust

Original trust agreement	$1,200.00
Settlement expenses***	200.00
	$1,400.00

Saving – $3,500.00

* No state taxes applicable
** A reasonable estimate of costs for an estate of this size. Includes attorney and executor fees.
***Does not include trustee fees, as a beneficiary may wind up trust without a fee.

Reducing Taxes

An A-B trust (more on this later) takes full advantage of the $600,000 personal exemption available to each spouse. The tax-saving testamentary trust in a will performs the same function, but the A-B trust arrangement is simpler to set up and completely avoids probate. This is the sole tax benefit of a living trust.

Flexibility

Multiple marriages with offspring from different parents are much more common today. The living trust provides more flexibility in planning for the distribution of your property to all children and spouses. A living trust can be amended more easily than a will or joint ownership to provide additional flexibility. For example, spouses married for the second time may have three living trusts. The husband has a living trust for his separate property. The wife has a living trust that includes her separate property. If they are in a community property state (see Chapter 10), they have a different trust with community property that was acquired during the marriage. Each trust can name beneficiaries for those assets only. With each spouse creating his or her own living trust, prenuptial agreements may not be needed or can be greatly simplified. Be sure to consult your attorney about naming a spouse to be a co-trustee of all trusts, as a trustee exercises considerable power.

How a Living Trust Works

The work of a living trust divides into two parts: establishing the trust and managing the trust.

Establishing the trust begins by asking your attorney to draft the trust agreement according to your instructions as to who gets what and when, with various contingencies unique to your situation. Many of the forms are standard, and your attorney may simply pull these paragraphs from his or her computer. The other elements will be specifically drafted to meet your individual needs. When you have reviewed the trust agreement, you, and your spouse, if you are married, sign the agreement and have it notarized. You are now in business.

Your first step in managing the trust is to transfer title to all of your property to your trust. If you and your spouse plan separate trusts, you both must follow the appropriate steps for your respective trusts.

It is critical to the optimum functioning of your living trust to have everything you own within the trust. No property should be in your own name. Anything left out of the trust may have to go through probate. There are some exceptions. If the value of the possessions outside of your living trust totals less than $30,000 or the possessions do not need a legal transfer of title, they can escape probate. A "pour-over will" may be written to collect any bits and pieces omitted or inadvertently left out of the trust. This property may go through probate if the total exceeds the minimum. The name comes from the fact that these odds and ends are "poured over" into your living trust. Finally, checking accounts are commonly left out of the trust for convenience if they total far less than $30,000.

If you set yourself up as the trustee of the living trust that now "owns" your property, you will notice few changes in how you manage your affairs. You can buy and sell securities in the trust. You can sell your house and buy another. You or your designated trustee can manage your property just as before, but you do it in the name of the trust. Some real estate may be easier to sell with you as the individual or joint owner. In such cases, simply transfer property out of the trust, sell it, and put the proceeds back into the trust.

No change in income tax or reporting requirements occur as a result of your putting practically everything you own into the living trust. As far as the IRS is concerned, your living trust is "transparent." The IRS sees through the trust to the assets and income they produce. You file the same personal income tax return as you did before establishing the living trust. The IRS does not require a separate return for the trust. Furthermore, you continue to use your social security number for identification.

Property transferred to your living trust remains accessible to creditors during your lifetime. Assets in a B-trust set up by a decedent are not accessible after the death of the spouse if that spouse takes the $600,000 estate tax exemption. (See pages 75 and 76 for information on A, A-B, and A-B-C trusts.)

When Living Trusts Are Not Suitable

While living trusts are useful for all the reasons noted above, they may be unsuitable for certain people or in certain situations. Here are a few examples.

Young, healthy adults may postpone establishing a living trust. A young couple's primary goals may be to provide a guardian, leave insurance death benefits to care for children or others, and leave their minimal property to clearly designated heirs. A will may support these objectives. A living trust cannot be used to appoint a guardian in the case of the simultaneous death of parents of minor children or in case a surviving spouse

is not able or willing to be the guardian. Another drawback is that trustee fees can mount significantly over many years if the person or couple lives in a state that does not permit the creator of the trust to act as his or her own trustee. When they are older and children are no longer minors, a couple may establish a living trust to deal with their greater resources and to avoid probate.

People with minimal property or assets that are owned jointly may not be candidates for a living trust because of the initial expense. If most of your assets are in the form of death benefits from an insurance policy, the proceeds may be directed to a beneficiary without probate. Other assets may be simply given away. These persons will not own real estate that requires a living trust or probated will to effect a legal change of title. An informal bank trust, one that is set up to **"pay-on-death,"** that is, when the balance becomes the property of a named beneficiary, may also avoid the need for either a will or living trust to transfer checking or saving accounts. In community property states a community property agreement may give all of a couple's assets to a surviving spouse. A few other states may have similar provisions. Before relying on one or more of these alternatives, be sure you understand any potential problems. If the problems seem too great, then consider a living trust that provides greater flexibility for transferring assets.

People loaded with debts, including, for instance, a sizable mortgage, may need the authority of a court for mandating decisions and should use a will, which will be probated at their death. A probate court provides specific cutoffs for debts and clarifies titles to property that are under liens or subject to payment schedules. A will to be probated will not avoid debts; that is the province of a bankruptcy court. But, disputed claims can be resolved and paid for in a probate procedure to leave property with a clear title for heirs. Using a will to clarify debt problems may be particularly beneficial if the decedent owns a business. A living trust provides no similar legal cutoff to possible future claims from creditors.

People who currently own little or no property but who expect to inherit property or to receive litigation proceeds should not use a living trust. A living trust consists only of the transferring of currently owned property title into the trust. If you expect to own property later, protect any assets now with a simple will. Later, when the property is in your hands, you may wish to set up a living trust. Or, you may set up a living trust to include currently owned property and write a will for anything not transferred to the trust. If you should receive property shortly before your death, the will provides a backup to the trust.

Different Types of Trusts

Trusts come in different shapes and flavors according to the size of your estate and your marital status. Typically, the different types of trusts break into three classes: A, A-B, and A-B-C.

Type A Trusts

Type A trusts are suitable for single individuals and married couples with taxable assets totalling less than $600,000. A single person with more than $30,000 in assets can establish a living trust and act as trustee in most states. The cost benefits of a Type A living trust over a probated estate are noted briefly in Table 5A on page 72.

A married couple with an estate of less than $600,000 may use a Type A trust because their estate would not incur a federal estate tax at the death of either the first or second spouse. For example, suppose Mary and John Doe own property worth a total of $500,000. If John should die first, Mary ends up with all of the property owned by the trust and takes over the management as trustee. No federal estate taxes are due because the taxable estate is valued at less than $600,000. Mary controls the value of the estate to keep it under $600,000 during her lifetime. At her death the value of the estate totals less than the $600,000 exemption level. Having only one trust simplifies management of trust estates.

Type A-B Trusts

Type A-B trusts may also be tax-saving trusts for married couples because they take full advantage of each spouse's $600,000 exemption.

In an A-B trust, a couple's living trust includes two subtrusts usually labeled A, for the wife, and B, for the husband. Suppose the husband dies first. The surviving spouse in her capacity as trustee takes over the management of both subtrusts. Assets in Trust B will be subject to an estate tax only if the husband's portion exceeds $600,000. In settling the estate, the Trust B is immediately irrevocable because the husband is no longer living. According to the provisions of the trust, the husband's portion remains in trust for his beneficiaries. The widow is entitled to the income from the assets in Trust B.

Further, she may be entitled to some of the principal under two conditions: (1) If income from her own Trust A assets are insufficient to support her former lifestyle, she may withdraw as many assets from the husband's Trust B as she needs. (2) Without having to establish a lifestyle spending level, she may withdraw either $5,000 per year or 5 percent of the Trust B assets, whichever is greater. The widow continues as the trustee of her own Trust A. If she is also the successor trustee of Trust B, which is typical, she is the one who decides whether income from her Trust A is sufficient to maintain her usual lifestyle. So, setting Trust B aside as irrevocable at the death of the husband has little practical effect on the widow's access to the assets in both Trusts A and B. One problem could occur if the beneficiaries designated in the husband's Trust B become alarmed that the widow, in her position as successor trustee, is draining assets from Trust B. The eventual beneficiaries of Trust B, possibly the couple's children, may figure they will be getting less than they anticipated and sue. While not likely, this possibility exists.

Trust B contains roughly half of the couple's assets and is entitled to the full $600,000 estate tax exemption. Later at the surviving widow's death, only the assets in Trust A are subject to an estate tax. For example, suppose John and Mary Doe have a living trust worth $1 million equally divided between Trust A and Trust B. At John's death, the $500,000 in his Trust B are protected by the $600,000 estate tax exemption. When Mary dies later, only the $500,000 in her Trust A are subject to estate taxes, and her estate pays no taxes because the $600,000 exemption protects them. If the couple had not established the A-B trust, $400,000 of their combined estate would be subject to tax when Mary dies. (See Box B in Chapter 3 for details.)

The A-B living trust arrangement provides the same protection for assets owned by a couple as a tax-saving trust set up under a will. The main difference is that the tax-saving trust in the will is a testamentary trust and must go through probate with its added delays and costs.

For most couples the single A-B living trust covers all bases. Only if either spouse owns separate property acquired before the marriage or inherited after the marriage is a separate trust needed. In fact the single shared living trust simplifies administration. While both spouses are living the shared property need not be specifically divided.

Type A-B-C Trusts

An A-B-C trust may be desirable if a couple owns more than $1.2 million of assets. In this case the $600,000 estate tax exemption available to each spouse protects $1.2 million of taxable assets but still leave property over the $1.2 million limit subject to tax. If you should be in this position, you need to decide whether the estate of the first spouse to die will pay a portion of the tax, or whether all of the shared estate in excess over the $600,000 exemption available at the first death will flow to the surviving spouse.

Estate taxes will probably be higher if all of the property flows to the surviving spouse. (See the box on page 53 for the difference for a couple with an estate valued at $1.6 million at the time of the first death.) Dividing the estate and paying a portion of the estate tax at the first death reduces taxes because two portions are taxed at lower rates than if all the excess property is taxed as one portion at the second death. The unified gift and estate tax schedule is progressive. The marginal tax rate for the first dollar over the $600,000 exemption level is 37 percent and escalates to a maximum of 55 percent.

Trust A will normally include those assets owned by the wife. Trust B will normally include those assets owned by the husband. Those assets over $600,000 remaining after both have died are transferred into Trust C. Division of a couple's property among the three trusts is arbitrary and may be changed at will while both are alive. If the husband should die first, his trust (B) will become irrevocable, and the composition of assets within his trust can no longer be changed. The three trusts are managed like the other types of trusts, with assets being distributed when first one and then the other dies. Taxes are paid on any assets remaining in Trust C. Once the assets have been distributed from all three trusts, the trusts cease to exist. Successor trustees for the trusts must be clearly designated.

Children's Trusts

You may not leave any substantial assets directly to minors. If you plan to leave a substantial part of your assets to persons who may be minors at your death or at the death of your spouse, set up a children's trust and designate a trustee to manage the resources for the benefit of the minors. When the beneficiaries reach their majority at age 18 (21 in some states), the assets may belong to them or some portion may be held in trust until they reach an age specified in the trust agreement. You may include the children's trust within your own, but if you should die before the children reach their majority, that trust becomes irrevocable and the problem of minors' interests continues. If the children reach their majority before you die, they receive the property outright.

Different forms of children's trusts may be subject to various conditions:

• If the children's estate is minimal and would be expended before the children attain their majority, you could leave it to a person you have confidence in, and he or she, in turn, will use the money or other assets for the child's or children's benefit. This person may be the guardian. Leaving the money directly avoids the complications of a trust.

• Leaving property to a children's trust calls for designation of a trustee. Avoid appointing the guardian as the trustee of a children's trust. A children's trust may be set up to delay distribution until each beneficiary attains some designated age. A child may be a minor at the time the trust is established and no longer a minor when the creator dies. For example, a child may be 10 at the time the trust is created, 27 at the time the creator dies, and the trustee distributes the property only when the child reaches age 32. During these periods the trustee or successor trustee may spend portions of the assets for the child's support or education.

• Instead of leaving specified property to individual minors, you could leave assets to a single trust for all of the children. But, numerous administrative problems argue against this "pot" trust:

1. Income tax returns may be more time consuming to prepare.
2. The "pot" trust may not be dissolved until the youngest child reaches majority or some other specified age.
3. The trustee's broad power may be misused to favor one or more children in the group. The flip side of this is that the trustee can spend more of the trust assets on one beneficiary who may need it for special health or educational needs.

With a living trust you need not take special steps to disinherit a child or other relative. The living trust is inclusive, not exclusive. If a child or other relative is not named in the trust, that person does not participate. However, to avoid the possibility that others might believe you "forgot" a child or other relative, you could name that person in a pour-over will, leaving him or her no property or else a $1 token bequest.

Establishing Your Living Trust

Once you have studied your estate planning options, you may consult with your attorney about which type of trust (A, A-B, or A-B-C) is best for you. Your compilation of assets using the worksheets in Chapter 2 are critical for this decision. You will need to name the trust. Use your own name for the trust. For example, "The John Doe Trust," if you are single, or "The John and Mary Doe Trust" if you are married.

There are four major questions you must answer as you establish the trust:

1. What should you put into the trust?
2. Who will be your trustees and successor trustees?
3. To whom will you leave your property (who will be your beneficiaries)?
4. How will your debts and taxes be paid?

What Should You Put into the Trust?

A single schedule, or listing, of assets usually suffices for a single person. A married couple may use a single schedule or several. Practically everything you own, either as a single person or as a couple, should be placed in the trust. The few exceptions are noted later. You might use one schedule to list the property belonging to the husband, another for the wife's property, and a third for their shared property. Persons living in one of the community property states should use separate schedules to identify their separate property. But in general, the fewer schedules, the simpler the living trust.

Identify precisely each piece of property to be included in the trust. Your house listing, for example, should include its address and its legal description (from your property tax form). List a bank account by its number and the name and address of the bank. Stocks can be identified by company, number of shares, and certificate and **CUSIP** numbers. (CUSIP is an acronym for the Committee on Uniform Securities Identification Procedures, managed by the American Banker's Association. A CUSIP number identifies each stock or bond certificate.) List furnishings by room, such as "Herman Miller chair and ottoman in living room." Jewelry should be described as precisely as possible. You may have an appraisal list and the property could be noted as "listed on appraisal by [name of appraiser] dated _____."

Transferring cash can be risky because it changes hands readily and does not remain fixed in amount. Because cash is likely to be a small part of an estate, it's better to keep it out of the trust.

Listing ownership of or interests in businesses may require an attorney's help, or you can simply list a solely owned business by its name, such as "The Friendly Record Shop."

Listing property on the schedule does not transfer it to the living trust. The list simply indicates all of the property owned by the trust. You must take additional steps to change the title of property from your name(s) to the trust.

Who Will Be Your Trustee?

You may be the trustee while you are living. At your death the living trust becomes irrevocable, and the successor trustee takes over the management of the trust assets. You should define what happens if you should become incapacitated—who is to decide whether you are capable or not and who takes over. Ordinarily, the successor trustee named in the trust agreement acts at your death or if you are incapacitated.

A couple may designate either spouse to function as trustee while both are living. At the first death, the surviving spouse will ordinarily be named as the successor trustee for the trust of the deceased spouse and continue acting as trustee of his or her own trust. At the second death, a successor trustee manages the dissolution of the estate. Include provisions if either or both spouses should be incapacitated or die simultaneously in an accident.

However, a spouse may not wish to serve as trustee. A trust offers a way out of dealing with badgering relatives looking for an early distribution of assets or charities looking for contributions. The surviving spouse may easily refer requests to the successor trustee. Even if the surviving spouse were willing, she or he cannot make the transfers because she or he is not the trustee.

You must always designate a successor trustee plus an alternative successor trustee to be assured someone will take charge if the successor trustee is unable or unwilling to act. A successor trustee takes over the management of your living trust if you are single at your death. For a spousal trust, a successor trust ordinarily takes over after the second death. The main job of the successor trustee is to distribute the assets in your living trust to the beneficiaries.

If you are single and choose not to be the trustee of the living trust, or if you are married and neither you nor your spouse chooses or is able to act as trustee, you must name someone else. Or you may decide at a later date to appoint an alternative trustee. As you and your spouse grow older, you may decide to shift some of the burden of managing your assets to the alternative trustee. Perhaps you will decide to travel extensively or to live in a moderate climate for several months each year. Somebody needs to "mind the store" back home. The alternative trustee continues to handle day-to-day management of the trust assets and will usually be paid a fee for his or her activities. The trust might include a provision that if the grantor believes he or she may be losing some of his or her acumen or judgment, he or she can turn over the management to the alternative trustee. A court judgment on his or her incompetency is not expected; rather, the turnover of management responsibility occurs voluntarily. A trust may be developed where only the assets requiring active management, such as a business, a substantial securities portfolio, or rental real estate are included, and a trustee is appointed immediately to remove any possibility that a grantor's impaired faculties might lead to a series of losses. But be aware that your choice not to act as your own trustee complicates the way the trust is drawn and administered. You will need to set up safeguards on the way the trustee may function, possibly ask for a bond and set up separate trust accounts to satisfy the IRS. Further, a separate trust tax return may be needed. Because the choice of a first trustee is so critical, check with your attorney if you prefer not to act in that capacity.

Who Will Be Your Beneficiaries?

Three types of beneficiaries may be specified: beneficiaries are those persons or organizations designated to receive bequests; alternative beneficiaries, also known as contingent beneficiaries, receive bequests if the original beneficiaries are unable to, for instance, if they have predeceased you; and residuary beneficiaries receive any property that is left over and is not specifically designated for either beneficiaries or alternative beneficiaries. A clause naming a beneficiary and what he or she is to receive may read: "[name] is to be given my [describe your specific property, such as stock, an antique rocker, or other property]." If more than one beneficiary is to receive divisible property, such as shares of stock, be sure to note the proportion of shares to be given to each or if the named beneficiaries are to receive equal shares.

Be sure to name a residuary beneficiary, even an alternative residuary beneficiary as final contingencies to allow for prior deaths or an unwillingness to receive property.

Identify the property that is to go to specific beneficiaries. You may refer to the list of property transferred into the trust and use the same identification for those items. Use the name, number of shares, and certificate numbers for stock, for example. Listings of property may be separated according to which beneficiaries are to receive specific items. When specifying gifts from your list of furnishings to go to beneficiaries, note all the possible beneficiaries. For example, you might note: "The king-size bed in the master bedroom is to go to my daughter Evangeline Doe, or if she is not living, to her oldest daughter, and to the First Methodist Church if neither is living."

You may wish to name a charitable organization as a beneficiary of the trust. Ordinarily, these bequests will be acted on quickly during the settlement of the estate. If a grantor should decide he or she wants to support a favorite charity, such as a boy's club, a sorority, or a hospital for a number of years, a trust provides continuing direction. Income-producing assets may be transferred to a trust and a fiduciary trustee appointed to administer the trust at the grantor's death. Specific amounts may be given to charities noted or a percentage of income may be distributed to avoid drawing down the assets to pay specific dollar amounts. At some time in the future, however, the trust must end, as the IRS will not permit a trust to endure forever. The only way to set up a permanent endowment is by creating a foundation with a long or unlimited life. If you wish to look into this alternative, check with an attorney. IRS restrictions on foundations are strict and complex.

Your interest in property owned jointly as community or shared property may not be given to beneficiaries. You should give these shares to the co-owner, your spouse in most cases. However, if you and your spouse own shares in XYZ Corp. jointly, you could specify that your interest in those shares (identified specifically) are to go to your children equally. Distribution may follow the second death.

If you want to give all of your property to your spouse if you predecease her (him), simply note: "All of my property, including any shared interests with my wife (husband) are to go to (name of spouse)." All your property may be given to others in equal shares by simply noting their names as beneficiaries. "All of my property is to go to (name two or more beneficiaries) in equal shares. If one should not be living, the others are to share my property equally."

Giving property to minors requires a follow-up step to provide a trustee for the property until they reach their majority. The simplest way to accomplish this is to leave property to minors in a custodial **Uniform Gifts** (or **Transfers) to Minors Act** trust (UGMA or UTMA). **Custodians** (acting trustees) follow simple rules for managing the minors' property until they reach their majority. At that point the property is irrevocably theirs, and they may use it with no strings. For UGMA or UTMA gifts, name both the beneficiary and the custodian. If you plan to delay the time when minors receive their property—for instance, you may give your son your share of a business when he reaches age 35—you must provide a separate trust and name a trustee to manage it. While such gifts can be arranged, they complicate the living trust agreement. Ask your attorney for help on this, or better yet, forget the idea of delaying the gift and make it available at your death.

Insurance policies should name the living trust as beneficiary. You may name minor children as recipients of the insurance death benefits to be managed by the children's trustee. You may choose to keep some of the insurance death benefits in the trust to pay taxes and expenses.

How Will Your Debts and Taxes Be Paid?

Depending on your total assets and how well you plan your estate, no taxes may be due at the federal level. Many states levy no taxes on the estate or the inheritances received by individuals, but a few do. (See Chapter 3.) If your estate will be liable for federal and/or state taxes, you should provide a source of cash and designate that it is to be used for paying taxes. You might, for example, sell some stock and move the proceeds into a money market fund. Or, you could leave instructions for your trustee to convert designated property to cash and deposit it in a money market mutual fund. Any money to be used for paying taxes must be a part of the living trust. State estate taxes will be paid by the estate. Inheritance taxes may be paid by the beneficiary or you may provide a net inheritance; that is, your estate will pay the tax due on an inheritance and give the beneficiary a net (after-tax) gift.

Not all debts owed on property within the living trust need be paid before giving the property to a beneficiary. You could, for example, give your house with its existing mortgage loan outstanding to your son or equally to two or more children. The mortgage goes along with the property. The property's net value—fair market value less the loan—will be used in valuing your estate for tax purposes.

After your attorney drafts the final living trust agreement and you are satisfied with its contents, you, if you are single, or you and your spouse sign the trust agreement in front of a notary public. You need not have witnesses to sign your living trust agreement. The notary signature and seal assures the signatures are truly yours.

Transferring Property to a Trust

Once your living trust is duly signed, you can begin to put its provisions into effect. Your first job is to transfer your property into the trust. You have already listed the property, but you need to change the title for property with a title to show the trust as "owner." Transferring property to the trust calls for changing the titles and account names for real estate, savings account, safe deposit boxes, securities, car, boat—any property to be transferred—into the name of the trust. Suppose you and your wife own your house jointly, as "John Homeowner and Jane Homeowner, husband and wife." You would execute a new deed, often called a "**correction deed**" to change the title to "John and Jane Homeowner, trustees under trust dated (month, day, and year)." Be sure to record the change in title with your local recorder of deeds. Using a correction deed avoids any taxes that normally accompany a sale. Further, the correction deed (or equivalent) is revocable, as are other parts of the living trust. If your state does not permit correction deeds, your attorney will know the correct alternative. Because of the complexities of real estate transfer in some jurisdictions, you should ask your attorney for help. There may be other snags as well. Some lenders will not permit a trust to hold title to real estate on which they hold a mortgage. Other mortgage lenders resell loans to a secondary agency that will not accept trusts as owners. You can avoid this roadblock by switching title back to you and/or your spouse until the loan is complete. Then transfer title to the trust.

Send your stock certificates, bonds, or other securities to the transfer agent and request a change in ownership. If you keep securities "in street name" with your broker, switch the beneficial interest designation to your trust. Stocks "in street name" are held in safe keeping by a broker, but certificates are not issued. Instead the name of the owner, known as "the holder of the beneficial interest," is identified in the firm's computer but is not named on the register of shareholders by the corporation.

Noted earlier were short instructions for changing the title to your house from your name or the joint names of you and your spouse to the trust. Other property with a title; that is, you and/or your spouse are named as owners, must have the titles changed. Already noted are directions for changing the names on stock certificates, bonds, mutual fund accounts, and bank accounts. Convenience checking accounts may be left out of the trust due to their small size and the likelihood of their being jointly owned. Other property in your name may be a safe deposit box and various cars, boats, or other vehicles. Unless all of this property is reregistered in the name of the trust, the trustee or successor trustee will have no power to manage or disperse the property at death. You will presumably continue to manage the property as trustee during your lifetime.

Insurance policies, various deferred income plans, Keogh plans, and Individual Retirement Accounts need not be reregistered, but you should change their listed beneficiary from you or your spouse to your living trust.

Property such as a life insurance policy that has a defined beneficiary should be changed to show the living trust as the beneficiary and the previous beneficiary as the contingent beneficiary. You need not change any other part of the policies; just change the beneficiary to the trust. The simplest way to do this is to advise the insurance company, for example, that "the beneficiary should be changed to read _____." Other property with a beneficiary, such as annuities, Individual Retirement Accounts, Keogh plans, 401(k) or

403(b) plans, profit-sharing plans, pensions, and ESOPs, should be similarly changed, such as "the beneficiary of [name of account] is changed to read_____." When transferring an IRA, Keogh, or other qualified plan, be sure to transfer only the beneficial interest. Changing actual ownership could trigger a sale or outright distribution, which the IRS could consider as a taxable withdrawal. A change in beneficiary is not a change of ownership.

If you own property jointly with anyone other than your spouse, ask for help from an attorney, or from a title company if the property is real estate. Problems may revolve around determining exactly what you own. Unless these definitions are resolved, you may not be able to transfer a partial interest in the property to the trust.

Business interests can be transferred to beneficiaries more easily through a living trust than through a will. A long, drawn out probate could do irreparable harm to a business. Adding a sole proprietorship business to a living trust calls only for a listing of the name. However, if property is owned in the name of the business, title to that property must be changed to show the living trust as owner.

Transferring a wholly-owned corporation into the trust is a bit more complicated. Corporate resolutions authorizing the transfer must be approved by the board of directors and noted in the official minutes. Any property held in the name of the corporation must be reregistered in the name of the trust and stock certificates must be reissued showing the ownership to be the living trust.

Transferring an interest in a partnership or a business owned by several persons can create many problems. If you are in this position, you will need legal help to assure that a partnership agreement permits a transfer of partial ownership to a trust and to implement all of the needed steps for getting approval and changing documents. Even though the process may be time consuming and costly, you cannot afford to have a large chunk of your property outside your trust. If you don't change ownership to the trust, many of the same problems will surface later in probate court with long delays and higher costs.

Motor vehicles are often left out of a living trust to avoid problems with state registration and possibly with your casualty insurance carrier. Title to a motor vehicle can be transferred informally to a son, daughter, or other person as a gift. The vehicle never surfaces in a will and avoids probate.

Copyrights, patents, promissory notes, and miscellaneous property with a title can be transferred into the trust, but you may need help from your attorney. Unless these odd bits of property are treated with the respect they deserve, they may have to be transferred later at considerable expense and delay through probate court.

Nontitled property, such as furniture, Chinaware, and silver may be simply listed as belonging to the trust. Or, you may include a note in a Letter of Final Instructions that a particular individual is to be given designated pieces of property. While this statement of your wishes carries no legal clout, trustees will usually follow your directions.

Changing or Ending Your Living Trust

A single person may amend or revoke his or her own living trust at any time. Both spouses must concur and take steps together to amend or revoke a marital Trust A, Trust A-B, or Trust A-B-C. When one spouse dies, his or her trust is irrevocable and cannot be amended. The surviving spouse acting as successor trustee of the decedent's trust may manage it according to its provisions, but he or she cannot change it. The surviving spouse may change his or her own trust in any way he or she wishes, or revoke it.

You amend a living trust by attaching a written document noting the changes, additions or deletions. The separate document first identifies the name of the trust and states the date of the amendment. Changes are made by paragraph number and a simple statement, as "The following is added to the trust at paragraph No. _____" or "The following is deleted from the trust at paragraph No. _____." The document noting changes must be signed by you or you and your spouse before a notary.

Simple amendments to add or delete a beneficiary, change a listing of property, change a trustee or successor trustee, or add or delete titled property may occur often and are expected. You can make these simple changes yourself by employing a notary to witness your signatures. Do not attempt to alter parts of the original trust agreement by writing over or retyping portions. Alterations might be challenged at some later time. If your list of property includes some phrase, such as "and property that might be acquired later," you will not need to document each addition of nontitled property.

You may at some point need to make changes so significant that it will be easier to revoke an existing living trust and start over than to write numerous amendments. If so, use the same name for the new trust, and then reregistering titled property will not be necessary.

If you elect to end an existing living trust, you must transfer title to all of the property noted in the trust back to original owners. Revoking a living trust returns everything to its original status. If titled property is to be changed, consider the possible effect of gift taxes, as only gifts between spouses are not taxable. Gifts of less than $10,000 to anyone are not taxable.

Can You Write Your Own Living Trust?

A number of books and even a software program are available with the stated mission of helping you develop a living trust agreement without consulting an attorney. Sample forms with blanks to be filled in appear adequate for simple trusts and seem to satisfy the varied requirements of different states. But unique problems may not be anticipated in the standard forms. Particular problems may arise from the transfer of business interests, for example. It is preferable to have a lawyer draw up your living trust to guarantee that there are no errors or omissions.

Consulting and/or using these standard forms can be helpful.

First, finding and supplying all of the information asked for on the forms will stimulate your thinking about who you will name as beneficiaries and trustees and help you gather other information. The information you put on the forms will provide an attorney, if you choose to consult one, with all or most of the information he or she needs to complete your living trust agreement. Second, you may complete your living trust agreement using the forms and then ask an attorney to review it. If your estate is near the $600,000 or $1.2 million tax limits for single and spousal trusts respectively, spending a few hundred dollars for a check on your work makes sense.

Conclusion

A living trust may well be the preferred method for conveying your property to beneficiaries at death. You should make this decision only after a thorough review of the possibilities. Once a trust agreement is prepared, keep it in a safe place. The location of the trust agreement will be one of the items noted in your Letter of Final Instructions. Working copies of the agreement can be kept handy, as you may find it necessary to make changes in the trust agreement frequently, possibly several times a year.

CHAPTER SIX

Trusts

KEY TERMS IN THIS CHAPTER

charitable remainder trust   *actuarial value*
annuity trust   *reversionary trust*
remainder interest   *spendthrift trust*
unitrust   *life interest*
pooled income trust   *Q-TIP trust*

You have already been introduced to two extremely useful trusts to help you in planning your estate. The tax-saving testamentary trust (Chapter 4) fully utilizes each of a couple's individual estate tax exemption of $192,800, equivalent to the tax on a taxable estate of $600,000. A similar marital trust, also called an A-B trust, utilizes each spouse's $192,800 estate tax exemption when the living trust is chosen for distributing your estate.

This chapter looks at other trusts that may be useful in distributing assets at death or reducing the tax on your estate—and may include a deduction from your current income tax.

Caution: Trusts can be tricky. Preparing them requires precise language to be sure they do not run afoul of the tax code, and thus, fail to achieve the purpose for which they were conceived. Following are brief definitions of various trusts and the conditions under which they might be useful. Do not under any circumstances attempt to put together one or more of these trusts on your own. You need expert counsel and assistance to set them up properly.

Charitable Remainder Trusts

Created as a result of the Tax Reform Act of 1969, the various forms of **charitable remainder trusts** differ slightly in how they are drawn up and how income is distributed during the lifetime of the creator(s) or donor(s). In general, a charitable remainder trust accomplishes three objectives:

1. It excludes from your estate the value of any property you may contribute to an acceptable charity after your death through the trust.

2. By paying you an annuity out of the dividends or interest it earns, the trust provides a continuing source of income during your lifetime. At your death, the residual of the trust goes to the charity.

3. It offers you an escape from a "locked in" position with respect to capital gains taxes. If you have held stocks or real estate for many years and values have greatly appreciated, selling would generate a huge capital gains tax. Placing those profits in a charitable remainder trust offers a way out while also letting you contribute to a good cause.

There are several types of charitable remainder trusts. Which one is right for you depends on how much money you wish to put into the trust and how much income you want to earn from it.

An **annuity trust** requires the distribution of a minimum of 5 percent of the fair market value of the assets at the time the trust is established and once every year thereafter (hence the name). As the payment is exactly 5 percent and the amount does not change, the annuity remains fixed.

Here is an example of how an annuity trust functions:

Harry G. is sitting on a portfolio of securities with a current market value of $100,000 and a cost basis of $50,000—that is, it has appreciated 100 percent. On the basis of their current value, the $2,000 in dividends from the growth stocks provide only a 2-percent yield. Harry would like to increase the yield. He would also like to avoid a capital gains tax on the 100-percent appreciation. If he sold the stocks, he would report a capital gain of $50,000 ($100,000 net sale less $50,000 cost basis). At a marginal tax rate of 33 percent (federal only), his tax bill would be $16,650. No state income tax is due because Harry lives in the State of Washington, which has no income tax. Instead of selling the stocks, he decides to give the $100,000 in securities to his alma mater in an annuity trust. Income jumps to a taxable fixed rate of 5 percent or $5,000 per year as part of the annuity trust. Based on the appreciated value Harry gets an immediate tax deduction of $53,000, which at his marginal income tax rate of 33 percent yields a tax benefit of about $18,000. Combined with the $16,650 benefit from avoiding the capital gains tax, his gift costs him only $15,350, based on his original cost. For this he receives a fixed income of $5,000 per year for life. At Harry's death the **remainder interest** of the gift goes to the university for a further saving of estate taxes that would otherwise be due. A remainder interest is the amount of money left in the trust at Harry's death. The amount of the remainder interest depends on how long Harry lives and the earnings from the trust assets.

The amount of a current deduction for many types of charitable gifts varies according to the donor's age, the amount of income to be paid, and the rate of interest used to figure benefits. These variations are complex. Since 1989, the Treasury has been revising rates monthly. Figures in the examples may vary from current rates.

A **unitrust** is also a charitable trust that requires the distribution of at least 5 percent of the assets of the trust as they are revalued yearly. It differs from an annuity trust in that if the income from the assets, without considering capital gains, falls below 5 percent of the assets, only the income need be distributed. The principal may not be distributed. However, in some unitrusts, a "catch up" provision may permit added payments in later years to make up for years when less than the 5-percent minimum was paid from income only. A charitable deduction is allowed based on the present value of the remainder interest that will go to the university or other approved charity at the donor's death. At the time the unitrust is established the donor may choose between a high charitable deduction (with a low income payout) or a high annual return (with a high income payout). The higher the payout rate, the smaller the allowed deduction. Treasury regulations control the amount of the deduction, and it changes monthly.

Pooled income trusts transfer property to a pooled income fund. Ordinarily, contributions to a pooled income trust must be in cash or in the form of readily marketable securities that can be pooled with similar contributions from other donors. Contributors gain a life interest in the pooled income fund and receive an annual income dependent on the trust's rate of return for the year. You may choose from among several pooled income trusts. One may emphasize income. Another may aim for a balance between growth and income .

One feature of the pooled income trust is the small initial and continuing amounts that are accepted. Ordinarily, charitable remainder trusts set up with universities begin at $50,000 to $100,000. With a pooled income trust initial donations may be as small as $5,000 with additional payments of at least $1,000. Amounts vary from one charitable organization to another. Income payments may be yearly or more often at the option of the trustee. Here is an example of a college offering two pooled trust funds:

Wells College, a women's college in Aurora, New York, depends heavily on endowments and actively solicits contributions. It offers a life income plan with two pooled income options. (See Table 6A on page 90.)

Pooled Fund I is designed to produce high levels of current income paid out quarterly to cash donors. The yield to new donors as of November 6, 1989, was 8.32 percent. The investment vehicle used is the State Street Common Trust Fund, a portfolio of high grade corporate bonds designed to achieve a high annual yield commensurate with minimum risk and stability of future income. Gifts of cash only are accepted for Pooled Income Fund I.

Pooled Fund II is designed to produce some growth in principal as well as high levels of current income. Payments are made quarterly to donors who have contributed either cash or appreciated securities. The investment vehicles for Pooled Fund II are a mix of high grade stocks and bonds, specifically State Street Equity for Charitable Trust (36 percent) and the Fixed Income Fund for Charitable Trusts (64 percent). Pooled Fund II had a yield to new donors of 7.66 percent as of November 6, 1989. Gifts to this fund should be made in cash or readily marketable securities that are not tax exempt. The percentages and amounts of deductions allowed for an assumed $150,000 contribution and the payout rates are tabulated in the accompanying table.

The figures noted in Table 6A represent a typical example only. Markets change daily

TABLE 6A—Summary of Wells College Pooled Income Funds

Factors: Two lives, ages 65 and 72
Post 4/89 actuarial tables
Principal donated—$150,000
Note: Rates and percentages change daily. This is a typical example only.

	Pooled* Income Fund I	Pooled* Income Fund II
Current income rate	8.32%**	7.66%**
Percentage deductions		
Joint-life beneficiary	25.4%	27.9%
One-life—65	33.8%	36.2%
One-life—72	44.2%	46.6%
Dollar amount reductions		
Joint-life beneficiary	$38,087	$41,795
One-life—65	50,712	54,243
One-life—72	66,345	69,903
Quarterly income—joint	$1,426.50	$3,447

   Charitable deductions allowed when computing income taxes are based on a complex formula by the IRS and include life expectancy and interest rates on contributed assets. For example, 25.4 percent for joint-life beneficiary under Pooled Income Fund I reflects life expectancy for either member of a couple. One person's life expectancy from age 72 is less than at 65; thus, the deduction is greater because less income is expected to be paid to the beneficiary prior to death when the remainder of the trust amount reverts to the charitable institution. Dollar amounts of deductions are the percentages allowed for each beneficiary alternative multiplied by the amount of the gift. For example, 25.4 percent of $150,000 principal is $38,087, with allowance for rounding.
   Differences between Pooled Income Funds I and II indicate that less income is due to be paid out from Fund II; thus, deduction percentages and dollar amounts are greater.
Courtesy Wells College, Aurora, New York

* State Street Bank & Trust Co.
** Variable

and interest rates exhibit uncharacteristic volatility, so an estimate prepared the next day or next year would yield different results. The planned gifts department of major universities maintain a computer program that generates possibilities quickly and precisely.

If you are considering a gift to your alma mater or to some other acceptable charitable organization, such as a nonprofit children's hospital or a museum, but want to maintain an income stream for the rest of your life, a charitable remainder trust could satisfy both objectives. University examples are used here because they offer help in setting up the trusts and aggressively seek out donors. No part of the charitable remainder trust enters into the valuation of your estate. At the death of the last beneficiary the charitable organization takes title to the assets. Nothing remains from this contribution to be distributed to beneficiaries.

When you contribute to a charitable remainder trust, you gain an immediate income tax deduction for the **actuarial value** of the gift. Actuarial value is an amount viewed statistically for risks related to life expectancy. The deduction depends on the age of the beneficiaries; the younger they are, the less is the actuarial value because they can be expected to live longer than older beneficiaries. You may provide for one- or two-life income beneficiaries. You need not be among the beneficiaries to receive income for life. They could include a spouse, parent, child, or friend. However, the younger the ages of the beneficiaries, the smaller the immediate income tax deduction because of the actuarial valuation. Younger persons who have more years to live will receive more payments than an older beneficiary. Thus, there will be less of a remainder available to the charity and, so, a smaller tax deduction at the time of the gift.

This kind of trust offers you another benefit if you are thinking about selling appreciated securities. If you were to sell the stock, you would be liable for a capital gains tax on the appreciation. But if you give the stock to a university or other approved charity, you gain a deduction based on the market value of the stock at the time of the gift. This is a deduction from your income tax for the year during which you gave the stock. Your estate will benefit from a charitable deduction if it forms the basis for a remainder trust; that is, the deduction will be from your estate but the amount will be determined later following your death or the death of the last beneficiary. Appreciated stock that is readily marketable may be a part of a gift to establish a charitable remainder trust.

Universities tend to be patient recipients of gifts for the future. They are willing to set up charitable remainder trusts and handle the paperwork required to invest contributed funds, manage the investment at no cost to you, pay quarterly or annual payments to beneficiaries, and wait to receive the bulk of the capital gift years later. Typically, a university or college may offer two or more options among the commingled pooled funds.

Your gift to charity need not be only in the form of cash or securities. Giving your house to a charity can yield three benefits:

1. You may continue to live in the house until you elect to move out or at your death.

2. You gain an estate tax deduction for the value of the gift that will be determined later based on actuarial rates that are in turn determined by your age and the age of your spouse.

3. The charity pays you an annuity based on your age and the appraised value of your house.

In exchange for these benefits the charity takes over full title to the house at your death or when you decide to move out permanently. Your beneficiaries or heirs gain nothing from your house. Considering how much houses may have appreciated in certain areas, giving your house to a university or similar charity removes a big chunk from your estate. If the house would put you over the $600,000 tax-free limit, putting your house in a charitable remainder trust would cost you less than you might think at first. The term house or personal residence may apply to any property you own and live in from time to time. Your "house" could be an ownership interest in a cooperative apartment house, condominium, or a vacation home. Farms also qualify as gifts in exchange for an annuity. Universities are particularly anxious to gain access to residences through charitable remainder trusts because real estate generally appreciates between the time of the gift and the death of the donor. Annuities paid to donors tend to be conservative.

Reversionary Trusts

Reversionary trusts are also known as "Clifford Trusts" after a doctor in California who conceived the idea many years ago. The reversionary trust is sometimes referred to as a "take-back" trust because of its unique temporary nature. A grantor or creator of a reversionary trust transfers assets, usually some form of income-producing property, into a trust that is set up to extend over a minimum of 10 years plus one day. After that period the trust assets may revert to some other person other than the grantor and the trust ceases to exist.

A grantor has two main objectives in setting up a reversionary trust:

1. To shift income from assets he or she may currently own out of his or her income stream to another person(s). Income flowing to another person does not add an income tax burden to the grantor.

2. To remove the assets from his estate. The advantage of this trust is that it allows income to accumulate, often at lower tax rates, for the duration of the trust.

The role of the reversionary trust was significantly reduced following the Tax Reform Act of 1986. Prior to March 1, 1986, a person with income-producing assets, such as bonds, a rental house, limited partnership, certificates of deposit, or some other investment, could transfer those assets into a short-term trust. A favorite beneficiary

may have been his or her children while they were minors. They could receive the income from the trust and pay taxes on that income at their rate, which would be lower, possibly as low as zero. Using this stratagem, the children could collect a fund for college from what amounted to tax-free income. Any person with income-producing assets would pay less for his or her children's college education than if he or she earned the income, paid income taxes, possibly at high rates, and spent the after-tax money on tuition and other college expenses. After a minimum time of 10 years plus one day, the grantor of the short-term reversionary trust could take the property back. It reverted back to the grantor.

The Clifford trust became a popular instrument for financing college educations. It was so popular, in fact, that Congress felt the short-term trust was being abused, and they struck down the important reversionary feature. Even though its attractiveness has been sharply diminished, there are times when it may be used advantageously, as noted in these examples.

Short-term reversionary trusts may still be set up to channel income from assets to children for college or other purposes. But, the assets may no longer revert to the grantor, a father for example. They may be turned over to someone else, but it cannot be the grantor or the grantor's spouse. If the assets revert to the grantor, then the income from the trust is taxed to him and the assets remain in his estate. One exception permits the return of assets to the grantor if the income beneficiary of the short-term trust is a lineal descendent and dies before the trust ends.

Using a short-term trust could be the first of two steps to channel assets to a charitable organization. A reversionary, short-term trust could be set up to hold assets that would provide income to one or more children. They could collect this income to pay for college at some future time. At the end of the collection period, which must be a minimum of 10 years plus one day, the assets could move on to a university or other approved charity.

New income tax limits for children could frustrate this use of the reversionary trust. The so-called "kiddie tax" or federal income tax on minors up to age 14 currently limits tax-free income for one child to $500 per year. The next $500 would be taxed at the child's rate, which is currently a minimum of 15 percent. Any income received by the child over $1,000 per year is taxed at the parents' marginal rate, which could be 33 percent. After a child reaches age 14, all income after his or her deductible is taxed at his or her own rate, that is, the children's rate, beginning at 15 percent. Thus, the possibility of providing tax-free income to children from a short-term, reversionary trust is now extremely limited.

Another deterrent to the use of short-term trusts is the gift tax. Transferring assets to a trust where income flows to a life tenant will be subject to a gift tax on the full value of the property at the time of the transfer. Further, the annual $10,000 exclusion per donee (see Chapter 8) may not be used to avoid part of the gift tax assessed.

Short-term trusts may be used to serve as an alimony trust. An ex-spouse may be entitled to the income from the trust but not the assets. At his or her death, or if the ex-spouse remarries, the trust would be dissolved and assets would transfer to an acceptable charity. The grantor may not reclaim the asset; otherwise, he or she would be taxed on all of the income. If the grantor should remarry, his or her new spouse may not reclaim the assets in the alimony trust without incurring tax penalties.

A similar trust may be desirable for a child whose spouse dies prematurely. If the spouse is the sole breadwinner, the child may be left with one or several small children with a minimum income for their support. A grantor may set up a trust and transfer income producing assets into it for his or her child's continued benefit.

Spendthrift Trusts

If you have reason to believe that one or more of your children or grandchildren cannot or will not manage his or her inheritance responsibly, you may choose to leave the inheritance in trust with limitations, known as a **spendthrift trust**. Courts have affirmed the right of a grantor to protect an heir from the heir's own profligacy or "spendthrift" tendencies. You may also choose to set up a spendthrift trust to protect your son or daughter from wild spending by his or her spouse. Since the trust owns the assets, neither the heir nor the heir's spouse may touch them. Instead, the trustee, some fiduciary such as a bank or trust company, is empowered by language in the trust agreement to distribute income and/or portions of the principal according to the trustee's judgment. The trustee has broad discretionary powers and may not be bound by creditors' demands to expand the release of funds. For these reasons and to avoid a conflict of interest, avoid appointing some member of the family to be the trustee of a spendthrift trust.

A spendthrift trust may be set up in a will, or it may be set up as a living trust; that is, while the grantor is living. But the trust does not become effective until the grantor dies, and it then becomes irrevocable. Presumably, you as the grantor can control the distribution of income or assets to your children while you are alive. Special provisions may bring the trustee into the act if you and/or your spouse become incompetent.

In general, only income is distributed to the heir by the trustee, as the principal may be destined to go to some charity when the beneficiary of the spendthrift trust dies. Depending on the amount of income distributed, portions of the income stream may be added to the principal in the trust. A well written spendthrift trust will include a provision that no part of the principal may be encumbered as collateral for any sort of loan. The penalty for noncompliance with the trust's provisions by the beneficiary may be forfeiture of any further interest in the trust.

At the beneficiary's death, the remainder of the trust may be left to the estate, possibly for the benefit of the heir's children (the grantor's grandchildren). Complex tax problems may be encountered at this juncture, however. Don't attempt to set up a spendthrift trust without the help of a knowledgeable attorney.

Some states do not recognize a "spendthrift" trust. In case of a suit by creditors the walls you believe you may have erected to protect the principal assets could be breached. Typically, gambling losses will not be recognized as legitimate claims against a spendthrift trust. But, any federal tax claims levied by the Internal Revenue Service against either the heir on the basis of income received by the trust or income earned but not distributed by the trust cannot be avoided. The IRS as the ultimate creditor will not be denied.

If you set up a spendthrift trust, you may not earn your son's or daughter's undying devotion. If you were not able to educate your children to spend their money wisely, don't expect a trustee to succeed where you failed. However, the spendthrift trust may encourage the trustee to either help the beneficiary learn to spend more effectively or to earn income on his or her own. Matching increased income disbursements to higher earnings by the beneficiary might act as an incentive.

Generation-Skipping Trusts

Before the loophole was closed in 1976, a grantor could leave a **life interest**, that is, a lifetime benefit such as income from a trust, in assets to his or her children with the assets to go to the grandchildren at the death of the children. This arrangement either avoided or minimized the eventual estate tax because the children could use only the income from the assets. In 1976 Congress imposed a tax equal to what the estate tax would have been had it not been set up for a second or later generation.

Some possibilities do exist for transmitting benefits to a second generation, but they require delicate wording and preparation. Don't attempt any sort of generation-skipping trust without expert assistance. You might be better off to avoid the attempt and instead provide the second generation with assets through life insurance.

Q-TIP Trusts

An interesting acronym, Q-TIP stands for Qualified Terminal Interest Property. The

Q-TIP trust was created as part of the 1981 tax act and specifies the distribution of marital property following the death of a surviving spouse. The Q-TIP trust establishes a limited type of marital life estate that accomplishes two specific goals.

First, taxes on all of a couple's property are postponed until after the second death. Any amount of property may be left tax free to the surviving spouse by the decedent without incurring a gift tax. Generally a tax-saving trust incorporated in a will or as part of an A-B or A-B-C living trust will utilize the tax exemption available to each spouse, but a Q-TIP trust may still be needed to assure that specific property is distributed according to the first spouse's wishes following the death of the second spouse.

The usefulness of the Q-TIP trust will be eroded by inflation. Property identified in the Q-TIP trust will be valued as of the date of the second death, not as of the date of the first death. If a surviving spouse lives for many years, the value of a house, for example, could double or more to push the value of the estate over the $600,000 exemption limit and substantial taxes may be due.

Second, a Q-TIP trust can create a life estate for the surviving spouse that permits him or her to continue living in the couple's house. A life estate is some bequest that continues for as long as the beneficiary lives. When the surviving spouse dies, however, the property may go to heirs identified in the trust. The Q-TIP trust can be particularly useful when spouses are married for a second or third time and have children by previous marriages. A husband may create a Q-TIP trust allowing his second wife to continue living in their house after his death but gives the property to children of an earlier marriage(s) when his second wife dies. The trust prohibits the surviving spouse from changing the distribution of the property at his or her death.

Like all of these special trusts, threading a way through the maze of regulations and limitations is no task for an amateur. If you believe a Q-TIP trust can benefit your estate planning, seek out a specialist.

Other Minor Trusts

A Care Trust

Provisions to care for a handicapped child may be the objective of a short-term or other trust. Assets would be transferred into the trust, and the trustee would distribute funds as necessary to support the beneficiary. Assets to fund the trust may come from a settlement by an insurance company or a court judgment if the disability resulted from an accident.

If your child is handicapped or injured, you may set up the trust and manage it as trustee for as long as you are able. However, to assure continued support after you are either incompetent or at your death, you should name a successor trustee, probably someone other than a member of your family. Care trusts will ordinarily permit the expenditure only of income, although provisions in the trust agreement could specify conditions where the trustee could invade the principal. A need for special surgery, for example, might be such a condition. At the death of the beneficiary of a care trust, the assets of the trust may be distributed to other family members or to an approved charity.

Small Business Trusts

This option distributes income from a business to beneficiaries of the trust. If family members were to inherit a small business that you own either by yourself or in combination with one or more partners, the business might not survive. The trust permits a trustee to function as a partner or manager. The business trust may be set up as a testamentary trust in a will or as a trust to be implemented at death as part of a living trust. In either case the business trust becomes irrevocable at the grantor's death.

Leaving your business in trust calls for a number of decisions you should consult an attorney about. What will ultimately become of the business is one decision to be considered. While a trustee operates the business or works with other partners, income may be channeled to heirs. Such a situation offers only an interim solution. At some point the trustee must decide on selling the business either to a family member or an outsider. Proceeds from the sale would be distributed to beneficiaries according to provisions written into the trust by the grantor. If the small business functions as a corporation, stock ownership may be transferred to the trust and eventual beneficiaries may be given shares. Or, individual shares may be sold at various times to dispose of the business if that is the desired end. The trustee plays such an important role here. Make sure you pick one who understands your business and who can be trusted to do the right thing for your heirs.

Trusts Outside the United States

A trustee or executor may direct contributions to beneficiaries within the United States. However, direct contributions may not be made to persons or institutions outside the United States. A trust offers a means around this roadblock. If a person wishes to support a nunnery in Italy, he or she must establish a trust and direct the trustee of that trust to send money to the nunnery or another offshore beneficiary. Not only charities but foreign individuals may not receive direct contributions. If you wish to send money to family members in the "old country" through your will or living trust, you must first set up a trust for that purpose. The trustee may send the beneficiary a lump sum when winding up your estate. He or she may also send a succession of payments from income in the trust to one or more beneficiaries outside the United States.

Seek counsel if you are considering any of the above or other special types of trusts. You could easily run afoul of tax liabilities that could frustrate your desires. Gift taxes need to be considered when the transfer of assets to a trust exceeds the $10,000 annual gift exemption (see Chapter 8) or the law expressly forbids the use of the annual gift exemption. Transfers to a spouse are free of gift tax. If a couple is living together unmarried, they are not spouses and gifts between them are not tax free.

Even though you transfer assets to a trust, you must pay taxes on any income that flows from the trust to you.

As noted earlier, some states might not recognize a trust used as a protection against creditors. A state may not permit other types of trusts that may appear to frustrate legitimate purposes, including the tax on income. Check with your attorney before establishing unusual trusts that might conflict with state codes.

Conclusion

Trusts other than the living trust that replaces a will can be flexible and useful tools in planning for the distribution of your assets. You may use trusts to accomplish specific purposes after your death such as supporting a favored charity or clarifying the distribution of property following your spouse's death. Anytime you leave assets in the hands of a trustee other than your spouse, make sure you have full faith in the ability and integrity of the trustee. Five-sevenths of "trustee" is "trust," and the power wielded by a trustee is near absolute in the administration of most estates. Be sure you pick the right trustee.

CHAPTER SEVEN

Joint Ownership

KEY TERMS IN THIS CHAPTER

joint tenancy	severing
JTWROS	partition
tenancy in common	stepped-up value
tenancy in the entirety	cost basis
community property	nonspouses
Uniform Simultaneous Death Act	

Owning property jointly has often been called the "poor man's will." What could be simpler? You and your husband or you and your daughter own your house together. If you should die first, your husband or daughter inherits the house with a clear title—and no delays or expense for probate.

Jointly owned property with right of survival escapes probate, and this method of passing along property can be beneficial for two reasons: 1) Property immediately belongs to the survivor and need not wait until a probate court acts; 2) When attorney and executor's fees are based on the value of the probate estate, removing major portions of the estate, such as the couple's house, reduces the costs of probate. Nonfinancial advantages may also accrue from joint ownership, such as the feeling of unity between couples when they own something jointly.

Despite these advantages, however, joint ownership is not always simple, easy, or cheap.

Joint tenancy, which involves the right of survival, is the common way for two people to own property together. If, for example, you and your spouse open a joint checking account at your local bank, you may see the letters **JTWROS** in the account application. Those letters mean "Joint Tenancy With Right of Survival." If you die, your spouse becomes the sole owner of the account. No restrictions limit access to the account by either you or your spouse. You may deposit all of the cash or checks into the account, and your spouse may take all the money out. Simple, yes. Hazardous? Possibly. Here's a case where it led to trouble.

Hazel D. was 82, a widow living in a retirement home. Her daughter, Ellen, lived nearby and dropped in to see her often. Hazel's arthritis progressively restricted her activities. First, she couldn't drive. Then she had to give up the bus. Walking was difficult and painful. To avoid having to go to the bank, she had her Social Security payments and earnings from bank certificates of deposit paid directly into her account. The daughter frequently ran errands for her mother and would buy items for her from time to time. Reimbursement was inconvenient, so Hazel decided to make her daughter a joint owner of the account. The daughter could write checks on Hazel's account to pay for items she got for her mother.

Good idea? Not really. While the daughter generally was a careful driver, her mind wandered at one critical moment, and she struck a child who darted into the road as she was turning left at an intersection. The child lived, but faced extensive and costly rehabilitation for a broken pelvis, internal damage, and other injuries. The daughter's liability coverage on her car insurance did not cover the full cost and the child's parents sued for the additional expenses. The upshot of the unfortunate, and certainly unforeseen, incident was that the daughter's accounts were seized—including her jointly owned checking and savings accounts with Hazel.

All of the assets in Hazel's accounts were seized to satisfy judgments resulting from the accident. Shortly after the incident, Hazel's health deteriorated, and she could no longer continue living in the retirement home. Without resources she was relegated to a nursing home that accepted Medicaid patients, a move she had hoped to avoid.

Who was at fault? Nobody really. But accidents can happen. A more reasonable course of action for Hazel would have been to create a Durable Power of Attorney for her daughter. The power of attorney would have enabled Ellen to write checks on her mother's account to pay for goods and services she wanted, but it would not have given her ownership interest in the assets as a joint tenant. Joint ownership should be limited to convenience checking accounts or home ownership between spouses.

How to Make Joint Ownership Work

Tenancy in common is a slightly different method for holding assets jointly. While assets owned jointly with right of survival automatically become the property of the survivor, assets held as tenants in common do not. That is, there is no right of survivorship for a joint owner in a tenancy in common agreement. A deceased co-owner's interest in property held in a tenancy in common becomes a part of the estate of the decedent and passes to his or her heirs. It allows you the advantage of joint ownership along with the freedom to will property to whomever you choose. Some form of conveyance, a will, trust, or other valid agreement, is needed to transfer title of the undivided joint interest to the other tenants in common or to someone else.

Tenancy in the entirety is a third form of joint ownership limited exclusively to spouses and primarily used for owning real property jointly. In some states tenancy in the entirety is the only form of joint ownership by which spouses may own real estate together. This distinction is a holdover from English law that considered two married persons as one unit or an "entirety." The right of survivorship remains. Neither person acting alone may end or change the ownership in a tenancy in the entirety; both signatures are required. And the property cannot be divided or a portion given to someone else. When husband and wife own a house as tenants in the entirety, the survivor owns the house by right of survivorship. This distinction is important in tracing legal ownership through title searches. Property inherited through a tenancy in the entirety is not available to creditors of the deceased co-owner unless he or she specifically encumbered the title.

Community property may be jointly owned by spouses in equal shares in nine states—Arizona, California, Idaho, Louisiana, Nevada, New Mexico, Texas, Washington, and Wisconsin. These states consider that marriage partners create a "community" and are equal owners of property acquired during the marriage. The different states handle community property somewhat differently, and laws in each state may vary. The marital deduction for estates was created to equalize the rights of spouses in the noncommunity property states. (See Chapter 10 for a detailed discussion of community property.)

Other ways to own property jointly are through partnerships, syndicates, and joint ventures. If you wish to learn more about these three additional ways to own property jointly, consult an investment counselor (stockbroker), or a financial planner.

If you enter into a joint ownership, be sure you understand what form of joint ownership it is so you don't run into legal problems. If you and your wife move to a new locality, for instance, or decide to change banks, the forms you sign to set up a joint bank account have already been through a legal review and you can rely on them. Read the small print to understand your rights and the details of the arrangement.

Joint Ownership Problems

Owning property jointly with right of survivorship automatically transfers title to a survivor. But what if there is no survivor? Suppose John and Mary Smith are both killed in an airplane crash. What happens to the couple's jointly owned property?

In the absence of a valid will or trust, each is considered to have survived the other momentarily under definitions in the **Uniform Simultaneous Death Act** (USDA). So, two estates are created with the property equally divided. Unfortunately, this result may double the costs for settling the estates, as two sets of fees, administrative expenses, and possible taxes will be due. The USDA affects only property jointly owned prior to the cause of death; the couple's other property not held jointly is unaffected.

The USDA encourages the writing of a will or trust to override the provisions of the Act. A well-drawn will or trust will contain a clause that defines how jointly owned property is to be passed on to heirs in the case of simultaneous death. Not providing for the contingency of a simultaneous death is a major liability for owning property jointly without a will or living trust to provide for the distribution of assets.

Ending or "**severing**" any of the joint ownerships may lead to problems. If one joint tenant takes his or her property out of the joint account and starts a separate account, the previous joint tenancy stops. You can't, for example, sell your share in a condominium held as joint tenants to a another person. First, you do not have a transferable interest. Second, taking a share for transfer terminates the joint tenancy. If joint owners sell the entire property, then the joint ownership also stops. Severing the joint ownership does not affect how the jointly owned assets may be distributed. That decision is made separately.

Legal steps may be necessary if joint tenants cannot agree on a **partition**, meaning how the property is to be divided between the joint owners. If a court decrees the conditions of a partition, then the property is legally divided and the joint tenancy ceases.

When property is owned as tenants in common, one owner cannot unilaterally end the joint ownership agreement. A tenant in common may, however, sell or otherwise dispose of his or her interest without the consent of the other owner(s) even though the interest is undivided; that is, specific portions do not belong to each of the joint owners. The new owner of the interest then becomes a new joint owner in the tenancy in common. Interests owned as tenants in common do not automatically go to the other owner(s) if one joint owner dies. Each owner in a tenancy in common retains the right to dispose of his or her interest through a will or trust.

Joint owners of a tenancy in the entirety (limited to married couples) retain the right of survivorship. When one marriage partner dies, the survivor owns the property. In a divorce action legal ownership of a house, for example, will be determined by the dissolution agreement.

Second-death ownership can become a legal sticking point. If one joint owner dies, the other joint owner owns the property lock, stock, and barrel—no question. But what happens when the surviving sole owner dies? Joint ownership provides no follow through for ownership of the property. The surviving owner needs to take further steps to assure passage of ownership to property, particularly real estate. Clear title to real estate, even in jointly owned property, must be legally established and in writing.

George T. discovered the delays encountered in establishing a clear title.

George, a widower continued to live in the house he and his wife, Gloria, had owned jointly before her death. About eight years after Gloria's death, George decided to migrate south to a warmer climate. When he offered his house for sale, the real estate agent discovered in a title search that Gloria's name was still on the official tax roles as a co-owner.

"You don't have a clear title to your house, George," the friendly real estate broker told him.

"But we owned the house jointly, and she died. It belongs to me as the survivor," George said and added, "I've been wondering why my tax bills kept coming with Gloria's name still on them."

The broker explained that George owned the property by right of survivorship but that the title needed to be cleared to show him as the sole owner. Nothing is automatic. George was required to either clear the title in probate court or file a death certificate with the recorder of deeds. So, eight years later George dug his wife's death certificate out of his records and filed it with the county. A new deed removed Gloria's name as a co-owner. A title search now would disclose the death certificate, which leaves the title in George's name alone. No arguments arose about George's right, only that legal niceties must be preserved.

Unintended results may follow from joint ownership. Stories abound where jointly owned property ends up in the names of persons far removed from the original owners. Unfortunately, joint ownership can provide no contingency or follow-on direction.

The following story illustrates the importance of having a will or living trust to specify how jointly owned property will be distributed after both spouses die.

Ben and Harriet M. were both married before. Harriet was Ben's third wife. His two previous marriages had ended in divorce. Ben was Harriet's second husband, but she had been a widow for three years before their marriage. Ben's financial obligations to his former wives and children had kept him strapped for cash even though he earned a substantial salary as a computer programer. The couple lived in Harriet's house along with her two teenage children, a boy and a girl. Although she needn't have done so, she changed the ownership to include Ben as a joint owner shortly after they were married, as a gesture of togetherness and to initiate a true partnership.

Through a succession of tragedies, Harriet died in an accident before her two children had finished high school. Since she had not kept her property separate, she owned the house jointly with Ben at her death. He became sole owner of the house through right of survivorship. The rest of the couple's property, most of which had come to the union as Harriet's, was divided between Ben and Harriet's two children.

After a few years, Ben married again. Shortly after that, he died of an acute heart attack with no will or trust to guide the estate administrator. The house ended up as the property of Ben's new widow who had children of her own. Harriet's two children were left with only the small distributions from her other property following her death.

For a summary of the different forms of joint ownership see Table 7A.

TABLE 7A—Effects of Different Forms of Joint Ownership

Condition or Situation	Joint Tenants	Tenancy in Common	Tenancy in the Entirety
Right of Survival	Yes	No	Yes
Right to Sell Shares	Yes	Yes	No
Right to Divide	Yes	Yes	No
Creditor Access	Yes	Yes	Possibly
Included in Estate	Yes (with spouse, ½)	Only your share	Yes (½)

Tax Impacts of Joint Ownership

Tax effects of proposed actions may dictate estate planning decisions, and owning property jointly is no exception. If a house is owned jointly and the wife dies, half of the value of the house ends up in her estate, except in some states, New York being one. There, all jointly-owned property ends up in the estate of the first spouse to die. The same division applies to other jointly owned property, such as stocks, bonds, a boat, and so forth.

But a spouse's half ownership in a house can lead to complications at a first death. For example, if a house was purchased for $50,000 and appreciated to $200,000 by the time a husband died, $100,000 would be included in the husband's estate valuation. Further, his half would receive a **stepped-up value** of $100,000 while the **cost basis** (that is, the house's original cost plus capital additions) of his widow's half retains the original $25,000 cost basis—half of the original cost (no capital additions to affect cost basis). The cost basis of a house is its original cost plus any capital additions. Capital additions are anything that increases its value but are not routine maintenance. Stepped-up value is the estate valuation of an asset. As noted elsewhere, a decedent's assets are appraised for their fair market value as of the date of death or the alternate date. In the case of a house, its cost basis (original cost plus capital additions) is "stepped up" to the appraised value at the decedents date of death. That stepped-up value becomes the new cost basis when it is later sold. Any difference between the cost basis and net sale value is a capital gain or loss. Gains are taxable, but losses are not a factor in tax computations.

Later when the widow decides to sell the house, she must figure any capital gains on the two halves separately. Suppose the house continues to appreciate, and she sells it at $300,000 net after expenses. The half interest gained at her husband's death generates a capital gain of $50,000 (half of $300,000 less the stepped-up value of his half or $100,000). Her half generates a capital gain of $125,000 (half of $300,000 or $150,000 less half of the original $50,000 cost basis or $25,000). This is an income tax on capital gains—not an estate tax. See Table 7B for details of this transaction. Community property states do not abide by this rule. In the State of Washington, for example, a community property state, both halves of a house owned jointly by spouses attain the stepped-up value by state statute at the first death.

Here's another example of how tax laws might affect your decisions regarding joint ownership.

William F. and his wife owned their house jointly. Following her death, he owned it as the surviving spouse. After a few years of living alone as a widower, he married Edna but stipulated that his house was to remain as his separate property. When he was 52, he and Edna decided to sell his house and buy a condominium in Arizona. At the time Edna was 55. Over the years, though, the house had appreciated to an estimated $135,000 with a minimal cost basis. He wanted to avoid paying income tax on the capital gain at the sale by using the $125,000 once-in-a-lifetime exemption. But he was not 55, one of the requirements. He decided to make Edna a joint owner because either marriage partner qualifies if he or he is over 55 at the time of the actual sale of the property.

TABLE 7B—Tax Effects From Jointly Owned House

	Husband	Wife (Widow)
House Cost Basis	$25,000	$25,000
Value at His Death	100,000[1]	100,000 (No effect on estate taxes)
Stepped Up Value	$100,000	$25,000 (Cost Basis)
Widow Sells House for $300,000		
Sale Value	$150,000	$150,000
Cost Basis	(100,000)	(25,000)
Capital Gain	$50,000	$125,000[2]

[1] $100,000 included in husband's estate at his death.
[2] If the widow meets all qualifications, she may be entitled to a $125,000 capital gain exemption.

But there was one problem—since Edna would not meet the use and ownership requirements for three of the past five years, she could not receive the over-55 exemption. She had occupied the house as William's wife, but she had not been a co-owner for that period. For her to qualify as an over-55 co-owner with access to the $125,000 exemption, she would have to wait three years. By that time, William would be 55 himself, so there was no reason to disrupt his sole ownership and change the designation as his separate property. They postponed their move south and continued to live in the house for one more year. After that they rented it and moved to Arizona. When William sold the house two years later following his fifty-fifth birthday, he was able to take the $125,000 exemption because he had met the three-of-five year occupancy qualification.

Pros and Cons of Joint Ownership

Not all reasons for owning property jointly have legal ramifications. But if you elect to own property for reasons other than right of survivorship, you should recognize the liabilities, if any, of your choice.

Nontax Advantages of Owning Property Jointly

Family closeness may motivate married couples to own property jointly for the sense of security it creates. A feeling of partnership appears to follow for many families with a heightened awareness of unity, togetherness, and team spirit.

The convenience of jointly owned bank accounts, both checking and savings, makes practical sense for many.

Jointly owned property may be protected from the claims of creditors in a few states. Variations in the law are extensive. If creditor protection is important to you, check your state's laws. Generally, jointly owned property is subject to creditor's claims.

Minimal delays at death permit a joint owner to gain access to and use assets held in joint tenancy. Probate administration can delay the transfer and use of many assets, but jointly owned property becomes the sole property of the surviving joint owner and avoids probate delays because property jointly owned does not fall into the probate estate. Costs associated with the administration of a probate may also be less when substantial portions of the estate were jointly owned and passed to survivors outside of the probate estate. Executor's and lawyer's fees plus other administrative costs are sometimes figured as a percentage of the probate estate—so smaller probate estates equal fewer fees and less expense. But attempting to place large chunks of a sizable estate into joint ownership to reduce probate expenses could complicate other provisions and create problems. Part of your estate plan should call for a tradeoff analysis of the complications of joint ownership versus potential cost savings. Looking ahead could save both time and money.

Privacy may lead to a desire for jointly owning certain assets. Probate opens all information to the public, but the passage of jointly owned property to survivors avoids public scrutiny. Thus, retaining privacy may keep the value of certain assets from the prying eyes of possible heirs and/or creditors. Where privacy is important, using a living trust may be easier than owning property jointly.

Nontax Disadvantages of Owning Property Jointly

Loss of direction or control over what may happen to property owned jointly after one death can be a big negative. If you own property as a joint tenant, you cannot will or give your interest to another person either while you are living or through a will or trust. You no longer have the sole decision on how property may be managed, invested, used for collateral, or divested. Persons may enter into a joint tenancy while they're on good terms with each other, but if relations should deteriorate, handling joint property can lead to bitter disputes. A jointly owned business or ownership in a business may be appropriate while the joint owners are living. But at death an inept or inexperienced co-owner may disrupt normal management activities.

Joint Ownership of Securities

Spouses often buy stocks, bonds, or other securities, such as certificates of deposit, in both names. A couple usually owns these securities as joint tenants with right of survivorship. You can check the wording of the brokerage agreement you sign when opening the account. Under these rules either spouse may buy and/or sell securities, and certificates will be issued with both names on the face. Spouses may transfer assets between them in any amount without gift tax consequences. When securities carry both names, any change, such as the sale of the securities, issuance of new shares in a split, dividend checks issued, or proxies to be signed must have both signatures exactly as on the certificates and on the account. Carelessness can delay transactions.

In case one of the joint owners dies, the securities belong to the survivor; however, new certificates must be issued in the survivor's name. As part of the estate settlement the executor or administrator would not handle jointly owned securities. The survivor may request new certificates directly by sending the old certificate, bonds, or CDs to the transfer agent along with a death certificate. He or she requests new certificates in the name of the surviving joint owner. An easier way is to take certificates with both names to a broker along with a death certificate. The broker sends the documents to the transfer agent. Securities not owned jointly in an estate may be transferred similarly, but in addition to the death certificate, a copy of a will, living trust, or other document giving ownership to a new owner, must accompany the request for a name change.

Joint Ownership by Nonspouses

All of the rules that apply to married persons owning property jointly go out the window when **nonspouses** are involved. Even a couple living together but not married cannot use the rules for spouses. Even family members, a mother and daughter, for example, play by different rules than those applicable to a married couple.

Real estate owned jointly generates many sticky problems. A married couple living together in a house they own jointly splits 50-50 interests. In the case of an unmarried couple ownership depends on which person contributed the money for the purchase. In addition, a gift, and a possible gift tax, may occur between unmarried persons where a transfer of a joint interest between spouses would be free of any gift tax. Tracking the value of an ownership interest by who contributed how much can create a problem if one of the nonspouse co-owners dies. Unless an ownership interest is fully documented, all of the house value may be included in the estate of the decedent.

To avoid the unending list of problems afflicting unmarried persons living together, some form of agreement should be developed to define ownership of any assets owned jointly as joint tenants or tenants in common. Nonspouses may not own property as tenants in the entirety. For property not owned jointly, such as clothes, household equipment, stereo sound system, automobiles, and items owned by each person but sometimes used by both, an informal listing may suffice.

Joint Ownership Is Not a Substitute For a Will

Owning property jointly may serve specific purposes, mainly between spouses. Despite the old feeling that "joint ownership is a poor man's will," a truer statement would be that "joint ownership is a poor will." Owning property jointly is not a satisfactory substitute for a will or living trust for all of the reasons noted above and a few others as well:

1. You cannot put everything you own into some form of joint ownership. You are bound to overlook something, possibly something important. Any property not specifically owned jointly will, in the absence of a will or living trust, be distributed according to the rules of the state for persons dying intestate.

2. Property held jointly may be distributed under intestacy rules by the state in the case of joint owners dying simultaneously.

3. Property owned jointly will go to the survivor without question if there is no will. Various contingencies, such as potential heirs marrying, dying or having children, after an agreement to own property jointly could change distribution of assets. A will or living trust provides much greater flexibility for stating contingent bequests.

4. If estate taxes should be due, property going to survivors of joint ownership creates a void. No cash would be available to pay taxes unless heirs cooperate. A will or living trust can structure the distribution for minimum tax effects where direct inheritance through joint ownership affords no room to maneuver.

Conclusion

Owning property jointly may be easy and convenient, even required when married couples acquire real estate. But joint ownership may and often does create more problems than it solves. Approach any joint ownership plan with caution. If in doubt, ask for counsel before going ahead. A will or living trust may make a distribution of assets easier and less costly than joint ownership when a person dies.

CHAPTER EIGHT

Gifts

KEY TERMS IN THIS CHAPTER

appreciating asset	*imputed interest*
annual gift	*kiddie tax*
donor	*support*
donee	*net gift*
stock split	

Gifts and giving are powerful estate planning tools as well as a generous way of sharing one's assets. A rule of thumb for estate planning if you're over the exemption limit is—"Give it away or Uncle Sam will take it."

Gifts to Reduce Taxes

Before the tax code was changed in 1976 and 1981, gifts were taxed at only three-quarters the rate for that portion of one's estate that exceeded the exemption. Prior to 1976 the federal estate tax exemption was only $40,000. Thus, there were many reasons for giving property to heirs rather than allowing them to inherit it through a will or trust. However, the Unified Gift and Estate Tax Rate table currently in effect taxes both gifts and estate assets at the same rate. (See Table 8A on page 110.)

The $192,800 exemption, equivalent to the tax on $600,000, applies equally to gifts and estate assets. You could choose, for example, to make a gift of $1 million to an heir and the exemption would offset $600,000 of the gift. Of course, $400,000 would be subject to a gift tax at the unified gift and estate tax rates. Even so, giving real estate or some other **appreciating asset**, that is, one that continues to rise in value, before death could be advantageous. We'll consider a strategy later in this chapter. First, let's look at the annual gift exemption, one of the easiest ways gifts can reduce your taxes.

TABLE 8A—Estate Tax Differences

After First Death or After Second Death

Assume estate of $1.5 million, $300,000 of which is taxable and divided equally between spouses

At first death

Taxable estate		$750,000
Exemption value		(600,000)
Net taxable		$150,000
Rate		.37
	Tax	$55,000
Same at second death		$55,000
	Total	$111,000

Assume only $600,000 taxable estate at first death

Taxable estate		$600,000
Exemption value		(600,000)
Net taxable		0

At second death

Taxable estate		$900,000
Exemption value		(600,000)
Net taxable		$300,000
Rate 37% on		$150,000
	Tax	$55,500
Rate 39% on		$150,000
	Tax	$58,500
	Total tax	$114,000

$3,000 additional tax payable if total excess is carried over to estate of surviving spouse after first death

Annual Gift Exemption

Probably the most frequently used tool for reducing estate taxes is the **annual gift exemption**. During the routine preparation of estate tax returns, the annual exemption will be taken routinely when estates would otherwise exceed the tax-free limit. As a minimum, a $10,000 gift will reduce an estate tax bill by at least $3,700 and possibly much more.

Basically, you can give up to $10,000 to any other person, relative or not, each year from your own assets without paying a gift tax. That is, as a **donor**, you may give as many **donees** as you wish up to $10,000 each without paying a gift tax on the money. In fact, you need not even file a gift tax return to report the gift(s). If you are married and your spouse concurs, the pair of you can give $20,000 of your assets to any one person without paying a tax or filing a gift tax return. If you and your spouse choose, you may give up to $20,000 to each of your three children, for example, and your taxable estate would shrink by $60,000. If you made annual gifts of $60,000 to these same three children for five years, you could reduce your estate's value by $300,000 with no taxes, no gift tax returns, and no reduction of your $600,000 estate exemption. Note these further characteristics of annual gifts:

• Your gifts are from after-tax property. That is, you will already have paid the tax due on the income that comprise the gifts or that may have been used to acquire gifts other than cash. For example, you may have saved $10,000 from your income after paying any federal and state income taxes. That $10,000 is after-tax money and can be given to a son, daughter, other relative, or simply a friend. Similarly, investment income may have accumulated after taxes or as tax-free income from municipal bonds. In either case the money is free of any tax liability.

• You cannot deduct annual gifts from your income tax bill. As noted above, gifts are only from after-tax money.

• Recipients of annual gifts (donees) pay no taxes on the money. Gifts are from after-tax money and no further tax is due at the federal level. Some states may levy a gift tax, but most have changed codes to conform

with the federal gift tax code to simplify administration.

• No time limits prior to death apply to annual gifts. You could, for example, give $10,000 to as many people as you wish from your death bed, and the value of those gifts would be excluded from your taxable estate. But, you must give these annual gifts during your lifetime. Your executor cannot make the gifts for you after your death.

Originally, the purpose of excluding annual gifts from any estate or gift tax liability was to avoid the problems of taxing transfers of small amounts of personal property. Christmas and birthday gifts were excluded, for example. The value of any gifts, including transfers of property, was formerly limited to $3,000 each year. At that time up to $30,000 could be given in a once-in-a-lifetime transaction without paying a tax. Along with significant changes to the estate tax code, the law was changed to increase the annual gift exclusion to $10,000, and the $30,000 once-in-a-lifetime exclusion was abolished.

Congress has perceived some abuses with the $10,000 annual gift exemption. It is considering a revision that would limit annual gifts from one person to $30,000 per year. No action is expected soon.

Planning Annual Gifts

Once you have determined that your taxable estate will exceed the $600,000 limit per individual, or $1.2 million for a spousal couple, you can plan gifts to minimize estate taxes. Suppose your net taxable estate amounts to $1.5 million, you are married, and you plan on using an A-B trust within your living trust. The $1.2 million will be tax-exempt, $600,000 following the first death and an additional $600,000 following the second death. That leaves $300,000 over the exemption limit, assuming no capital is spent between the first and second deaths. Unless you take steps to reduce your total assets, your estate will have to pay $110,000 if you and your spouse divide the estate equally, or $114,000 if the excess over $600,000 is carried over to the surviving spouse's estate. (See Table 8A.)

One way to avoid paying $110,000 to the federal government is to give $300,000 away. You could give a total of $60,000 each year to your three children, or three friends, for five years to reduce your taxable estate to $1.2 million. Another alternative is for you and your spouse to give 15 gifts of $20,000 each to 15 different individuals. Or your spouse could take over the excess after your $600,000 exemption. Gifts in any amount between spouses are not subject to a gift tax. Later, within his or her lifetime, additional gifts by your spouse to others could reduce the taxable value of the second estate to $600,000.

Gifts of Appreciable Property

Real estate, stocks, and interests in one or more businesses can and often do appreciate in value with time. Another method of reducing one's estate tax is to give appreciable property to an heir during one's lifetime. If the value of a building lot you have owned for years is in the midst of a neighborhood undergoing redevelopment and threatens to appreciate enough to push your taxable estate over the tax-exempt limit, you could give it to your heirs.

Suppose you originally paid $10,000 for a two-acre lot on what was once the far outskirts of the town where you live. The state recently constructed a highway near the land. Further, your lot was included in a land use revision and was rezoned from rural to commercial. The possibility of a shopping center or business park developing nearby has raised the potential value of your two acres. If building actually begins in the area within the next few years, the value of your two acres could skyrocket. As an investment, it is cause for celebration; this appreciation in value is exactly what you have been looking for, of course. But what if an appreciated value of $50,000 puts you close to the tax-free limit. If you and your spouse were to die within the next several years, your estate would likely be liable for estate taxes because the value of your land would have appreciated even more.

What can you do? You can take the property out of your estate by deeding it to your son or daughter. If you have more than one heir, you could deed it to them jointly.

If you elect to give your property to your heirs, you must file a gift tax return if the value of the property exceeds $10,000. Since the property is appraised currently at $50,000, you will have used up that amount from the estate tax exemption of $1.2 million available to you and your spouse. But look what might have happened:

The two acres appraised at $50,000 today appreciates to $300,000 five years from now when it forms a key part of a proposed shopping center. If you had not given the property to your heirs at the time it was appraised at $50,000, the property would be included in your taxable estate at the fair market value of $300,000. Dividing the tax liability between you and your spouse, your two estates could have had to pay $55,500 each. For both spouses the total reaches $111,000. Annual gifts in the interim kept your total taxable estate within the $1.2 million limit. Thus, the early gift of the appreciating property avoided the substantial estate tax.

The Role of Stepped-Up Valuation

One point to remember, however: A gift of appreciable property does not gain the stepped-up valuation of property that passes through one's estate. Stepped-up value is the appraised value of property as of the decedent's death or the alternate date. Appreciable property gains the stepped-up value as a new cost basis when the property goes through the estate. Since gifts do not gain a stepped-up value, in the example above, the heirs would carry your original cost basis for the property of $10,000. If they sold the land for $300,000, they would be liable for a capital gains tax on $290,000—the difference between your cost basis and the net price for the property. A tax advisor would probably advise them to sell the property in installments to spread the capital gain over a number of years, but this is not an estate tax consideration.

Annual gifts also carry the donor's cost basis and no stepped-up value is available. For example, you may decide to give your son or daughter 100 shares of XYZ Corporation. You paid $10 per share when you bought them years ago. At the time of your gift the shares are valued at $50 each. Your gift amounts to $5,000, less than the $10,000 limit on annual gifts. You need not file a gift tax return, and thus, there will be no effect on your $600,000 exclusion. However, your son or daughter will maintain your cost basis of $10 per share. If he or she should sell them later, the difference between the net proceeds and the cost basis of $10 per share will be subject to a capital gain tax. If your son or daughter sells the 100 shares of XYZ Corporation for $50 per share, he or she realizes a capital gains of $4,000 ($5,000 net proceeds less cost basis of $1,000), ignoring transaction costs.

If the shares of XYZ Corporation had remained in your estate, they would have received a stepped-up value equal to their price at the close of the market on the day you died. Your son or daughter would inherit the 100 shares of XYZ Corporation with their value stepped up to $50 per share. If he or she then sells the shares at $50 per share, there is no capital gain because the sale price equals the stepped-up cost basis, again ignoring transaction costs. This is another reason why knowing the value of your estate assets is critical. Taking property through your estate saves your heirs from paying taxes and costs you nothing as long as your taxable estate is less than $600,000 or $1.2 million for you and your spouse.

For example, if you gave stock you bought for $10,000 that has now appreciated to $50,000 to your son, he would take over your cost basis. If he sold the stock, his maximum capital gains tax would be 33 percent for a tax of $13,200 (33 percent of $50,000 less cost basis of $10,000). If the stock passed to your son through your estate, it would receive a stepped-up value of $50,000. If he then sold it at that price, no capital gains tax would be due. But your estate, if over the tax-free limit, would be saddled with a tax liability of at least 37 percent for a tax of $18,500. The family thus benefits from the gift by a reduction in taxes of $5,300.

Giving Depreciated Property

Avoid giving property worth less than you paid for it. For example, suppose you originally paid $50 per share for 100 shares of stock in MNO Corp. The price has dropped over the years to $10 per share. You could give the 100 shares of MNO Corp. to a son or daughter, and they would carry the same $50 per share cost basis. They may be young or be earning a minimal income. Selling the shares at a loss would not benefit them as much as it would you. Instead of giving your son shares in MNO Corp. valued at $1,000 (100 shares at a current price of $10 per share), sell the shares and give him $1,000 in cash. You can use the $4,000 capital loss as an offset against other capital gains or other income up to $3,000 for one year with the remaining $1,000 as a carryover to the next year. Your son or daughter receives the same value, but your cost of giving is less.

A different scenario applies if your marginal tax rate is less than your son's (or daughter's). You may be retired and paying only 15 percent on income over deductions and exemptions. But your son is doing well and earning enough that he is paying 33 percent on marginal income, or in the vernacular, he is in the 33-percent tax bracket. Giving him the 100 shares of MNO Corp. with your cost basis of $50 per share would enable him to sell the stock and offset the loss against other capital gains or income up to $3,000 the first year and the remaining $1,000 the following year. His tax benefit would exceed your tax loss for a family gain overall.

Giving Appreciated Property to a Charity

Giving appreciated stock to a charitable organization can provide a double benefit if your income is being taxed. You can take the appreciated value of stock, for example, as a charitable deduction and the gift reduces your taxable estate. Here's a case to show how this works.

Several years ago Ms. Smith bought 200 shares of DEF Corporation at $50 per share for a total investment of $10,000. The **stock split** 2 for 1 and continued to appreciate until the value of the shares doubled to $20,000. (A stock split increases the number of shares without increasing the capital value.) Smith and her husband owned property that exceeded their combined $1.2 million taxable estate exemption. Instead of giving the stock to a relative, Ms. Smith donates the shares of DEF Corporation to the university she attended years earlier.

Here's what happens. First, Ms. Smith gains a deduction of $20,000, equal to the appreciated value of the stock at the time of the gift. Since she is in the 33-percent bracket and capital gains are taxed at the same rate as income, she avoids the payment of $3,300 in income tax ($20,000 gross less cost basis of $10,000 times .33). Further, she decreases the value of her taxable estate by at least $20,000. If she had retained the stock and it continued to appreciate until her death, she might have to pay even more in taxes.

Giving Your House to Your Children

Your house may be your most valuable asset, and there are several ways of giving it to your children and thus removing it from your estate. You could simply give the house to one of your children outright by putting title in his or her name. You could create a joint property arrangement if more than one child is involved. In any case you would retain the right for you and/or your spouse to continue living in the house for as long as you desired. You might, for example, decide to give up your house in the East or North and move to a more temperate climate when you retire.

There are several advantages to giving your house to your children:

• Giving the house to your children removes it from your estate so that future appreciation of the property will not put you over the estate tax limit or push you into a higher estate tax bracket.

• You might want to remove your house from your asset base to qualify for Medicaid if you should need custodial care in a nursing home. Moving your home out of your asset base protects it from being used up to pay for medical expenses.

• In those states with inheritance taxes, giving your house to children in your lifetime might help avoid payment of "death taxes."

Despite these apparently good reasons for giving your house to your children, there are also some negatives involved:

• Suppose you give your house to your son by changing the title. You have made a potentially taxable gift. Since the gift exceeds the $10,000 limit for annual gifts, you must file a gift tax return, even though you pay no gift tax immediately. If your taxable estate, including the value of your house at the time you gave it to your son, exceeds $600,000 for yourself or $1.2 million for you and your spouse, all or part of the gift might be subject to estate tax. Your $600,000 or $1.2 million exemption is reduced by the value of your gift of the house. If your taxable estate falls within the reduced limits, no gift or estate tax would be due.

• Suppose that your son is married when you give your house to him. The house now belongs to your son and his wife jointly, but you continue to live in it according to your agreement. Things go along smoothly for a few years. Then, your son and his wife get a divorce. He could protect some of the equity in their home in a settlement, but the value of your home becomes part of the couple's assets that might be negotiable in a property settlement. Your son could declare your house as his own separate property to avoid including it as an asset to be divided. Unfortunately, the concept of separate property that is acquired by gift or inheritance outside of the marriage community appears to be breaking down. Judges making decisions on property settlements may consider the value of property belonging to one of the spouses as divisible.

• An even more unexpected development could affect your house. Suppose your son dies and leaves all of his property to his wife. Within a reasonable period she remarries leaving ownership of your house to a couple who may or may not be compatible with you and your interests.

• You can't sell your house if you have given it away. Nor can you sell it if you have given your son a joint interest in it. If you should decide you want to move to the Sunbelt for your retirement, your son would have to give the house back to you before you could sell it. Giving it back could create a gift tax problem for your son. Unless you have title to your house, either with a free-and-clear title or with a mortgage loan outstanding, you cannot sell the house. You are also not eligible for the $125,000 capital gains exemption available to homeowners who are over age 55 and meet occupancy and ownership criteria.

• Giving your house to children voids the stepped-up value gained when the house passes through your estate after death. If you give your son a house worth $200,000 and your cost basis is only $50,000, he takes on a tax liability that begins with $150,000 and will likely increase. If your son acquired the house through your estate, his cost basis would be only the $200,000 or the appreciated value as of the date of your death.

Selling Your House to Your Children

Selling your house to your children may appear to offer some advantages. You would gain the benefit of the $125,000 capital gains exclusion if you qualify. You might structure the deal to take back an interest-free mortgage if your children do not have the cash. Regular payments would provide income to you, and the sale would be one way of spending some of the equity locked away in your house. However, the Internal Revenue Service (IRS) takes a dim view of interest-free loans. If they notice, the IRS will likely impute an interest rate, taxing you on the amount you would be receiving even though you do not actually receive it. A 9-percent rate is typical, although the rate of **imputed interest** can change.

Generally, giving or selling your house as part of your estate planning should be approached with caution. Make sure you understand the ramifications before proceeding. At times the gift can make sense and save money, but there appear to be more negative considerations than positive ones.

Gifts to Minors

When you give some of your excess property to minor grandchildren, you may earn a double benefit: you reduce the tax-able value of your estate to save on gift and estate taxes. And you help your children with the financial problems of sending their children (your grandchildren) to college.

How you do this may affect your gift or estate taxes. Your children's income taxes may also be affected if you run afoul of the **kiddie tax**, taxes levied on children under age 14.

Simply giving money or securities to your grandchildren is not a good idea if they are minors. Being under their state's legal age of majority prevents their making legally binding decisions. Stockbrokers shy away from dealing with minors because they have been burned too many times. If a stock sale generates a loss, the minor simply claims he or she is not liable because he or she is a minor and cannot make a valid contract. So, the broker must absorb the loss. The usual way around this legal obstacle is to give your children or grandchildren the money or securities in trust. All 50 states have adopted a Uniform Gifts to Minors Act (UGMA), and 25 states have adopted an additional statute called a Uniform Transfer to Minors Act (UTMA). The differences are minor. UGMA accounts are limited to cash, stock shares, bonds, and shares in mutual funds. The UTMA expands the list of acceptable gifts to include real estate, collectibles, and paintings. Both statutes enable you to transfer assets to custodial accounts for the benefit of minors. These are simple trust agreements and most banks, savings and loan associations, mutual funds and brokerage houses can provide you with forms that meet your state's requirements at no cost.

UGMA and UTMA trusts call for a custodian who operates as a trustee to manage the account for the minor(s). These gifts would probably be limited to the $10,000 figure for annual gifts but not necessarily. Gifts to a minor could exceed the $10,000 annual gift limit, and the donor would file a gift return. As custodian, you or your children could manage the investment of funds within the accounts. You could, for example, give a granddaughter shares in ABC mutual fund. Your daughter, the mother of your granddaughter, in her position as custodian, decides to switch the investment from ABC mutual fund to DEF mutual fund. As custodian she is empowered to make the switch.

The assets you transfer to the UGMA or UTMA accounts belong to the child or children irrevocably. At age 18 in most states for UGMA accounts and 21 for UTMA accounts, the assets belong to the children. They gain unrestricted access to the assets to use any way they please. You may have intended that your granddaughter use the money to attend a university. But if she decides to spend it on two years of traveling, she is free to do so. Neither you nor your daughter can restrict the use of the gift.

While you may decide to be a custodian, the long-term nature of UGMA and UTMA gifts to minors calls for a contingent custodian if you are unable or unwilling to act. Your son or daughter could be a custodian or contingent custodian. However, if the parent of a minor acts as custodian and dies before the minor reaches his or her majority, the value of the UGMA or UTMA account is included in the parent's estate. If you provide the money for the gift under UGMA or UTMA rules and act as custodian, the value of the gift will fall into your estate if the child should die before reaching his or her majority. You may avoid this contingency by appointing a friend as custodian.

If your daughter is named as custodian of a UGMA account for your granddaughter, she must manage the account under her fiduciary responsibility. That is, she must exercise prudence and good judgment in managing the assets for the benefit of the minor. Further, she may not use any of the assets or income from the assets for **support** of her children. Support includes the usual housing, food, clothing, and similar necessities. Some states even require that parents pay for their children's college expenses out of their own resources, rather than a UGMA trust, if their peers consider attending college as a normal activity. Otherwise, the custodian withdraws funds from the children's trust to pay for college expenses.

Support is a poorly defined concept. Even the IRS keeps its definition of support purposefully vague, deciding each case on its merits. Some jurisdictions consider normal support as sending children to public schools, and in those jurisdictions the costs of sending children to expensive private schools could be paid from a UGMA or UTMA account in some areas. Other states appear to consider that children are entitled to an education commensurate with their own needs and aptitudes, and with the position and financial capabilities of their parents. However, the U.S. Tax Court in one ruling accepted the position of the IRS that the cost of sending the children to a private school is an obligation of affluent parents. If you elect to pay for your children's or grandchildren's private school education out of UGMA or UTMA funds, be prepared to defend your decision.

Income Tax Effects of Gifts to Minors

While gifts through UGMA or UTMA custodial plans aim to help your grandchildren, they may burden your children through increased income taxes. As the Internal Revenue Code now stands, children under the age of 14 may earn only limited income without burdening their parents. A minor may earn only $500 tax free. Another $500 in earnings will be taxed at the minor's own tax rate of 15 percent. Any earnings from investments or personal services over $1,000 per year will be taxed at the parents' marginal tax rate.

After a minor reaches 14, all earnings after deductions and exemptions will be taxed at the minor's own rate, beginning at 15 percent. Thus, the custodian needs to exercise sophisticated investment tactics to minimize the tax liabilities on UGMA or UTMA accounts. Several strategies are available:

1. Cash may be invested in tax-free bonds or tax-free mutual funds.

2. Cash may be invested in growth stocks or growth mutual funds with the expectation that few dividends will be distributed. One caution: growth mutual funds may engage in internal trades that could develop capital gains. Gains from internal transactions are distributed yearly and could be substantial. Distributed capital gains and dividends are currently taxed at the same rate and could easily exceed the $1,000 yearly income level. One partial solution calls for investment in index mutual funds that engage in few internal trading practices.

3. Tax-free or taxable zero coupon bonds may be bought for small fractions of their maturity values. Early compounding would limit earnings while children are under age 14. Later earnings would be taxed at children's rates when they attain age 14.

One other tactic involving the educational use of Series EE U.S. Savings Bonds solves the kiddie tax problem. These bonds offer two opportunities worth considering when you give to minors to pay for school expenses.

Buy EE-bonds and register them in the name of the minor with a parent as beneficiary. All income paid on the EE-bonds may be deferred until the minor reaches 14. Then, the bonds may be redeemed, as minors are not restricted from redeeming bonds registered in their names. Taxes would be due on the interest accrued during the deferral period, but the rate would be the child's own rate, probably 15 percent maximum. The cash could be moved into a UGMA account managed by a parent as custodian. Cash invested for a higher return would be taxed at the minor's rate. A parent is responsible for filing the income tax return for a minor when required.

Instead of buying EE-bonds registered in the name of the minor, any person may give money to the parents. The parents then buy EE-bonds in their own name and defer annual interest accruals. Later, the EE-bonds may be used to pay for a child's tuition, books, and fees, and no tax will be due on the accumulated interest under the new law. Payments for board and lodging do not qualify for tax-free payments from EE-bond cash.

Only parents have the privilege of using EE-bonds' accrued interest for children's college expenses free of federal income tax. An income limitation applies, however. If the parents' income totals less than $60,000 at the time the child enters college, all of the EE-bond proceeds can be used with the interest escaping tax. The benefit fades proportionately when parent's incomes range from $60,000 to $90,000. When parents' income exceeds $90,000 none of the EE-bond proceeds escape federal income tax. All EE-bond interest escapes state income taxes. If a child declines to attend college or does not meet minimum grade requirements, the parents still own the EE-bonds. When they redeem them and spend the cash for any other purpose than payments to a college or university, the accrued interest is taxable.

Net Gifts

A **net gift** is one where the donee accepts a gift with the understanding that he or she will pay the gift tax due. As an estate planning device, net gifts may afford several advantages:

Giving property will reduce the gross value of your estate. Since the donee receiving the property pays the gift tax, your estate exclusion remains. Since giving property may reduce your debts or tax liability, your total financial situation improves. The IRS considers this improvement to be a taxable benefit. If you intend to make a net gift to anyone, ask your tax advisor for an opinion about any income tax liability that might be incurred.

If the net gift is property that earns income, such as a rental house, you are relieved of a tax liability. You also lose income, but this should figure into your decision whether to make the gift in the first place.

Giving property may save local and state taxes. You are also relieved of insurance or protection costs on the property.

A gift tax will cost less when paid by the donee. To reach the net gift value, the gross amount of the gift is reduced by the tax to be paid by the donee. The gift tax will be computed on the net value of the gift; that is, the gross value less the gift tax. To arrive at the net value after the gift tax, divide the gross value by 1 + marginal gift/estate tax rate. For example, suppose your nephew agrees to pay the gift tax on jewelry with a gross value of $30,000. Your unified gift/estate tax marginal rate is 37 percent. Divide the $30,000 by 1 + .37 or 1.37 to arrive at the net value of $21,898. The gift tax will be 37 percent of $21,898 or $8,102. Adding the net value ($21,898) to the gift tax ($8,102) yields the original value of the net gift ($30,000). Some documentation will be required stating that the donee accepts the gift under the condition that he will pay the gift tax due. As a practical matter, if you intend making a net gift, follow up to be sure the person receiving your gift actually files the gift tax return and pays the tax. Otherwise, you as the donor will be liable for the tax.

Why would you want to make a net gift? There are several circumstances in which it may be a good alternative.

• You may not be willing to pay the gift tax on property you want to give away. Or an eventual heir may be interested in property now rather than later, but you would prefer not to pay the gift tax on it. The estate could pay the tax out of estate assets later. However, if the recipient accepts the responsibility for paying the tax, you could gain the advantages noted above with no out-of-pocket expense.

• You might prefer to transfer property and pay a gift tax now for a variety of estate planning reasons, but you may not have the cash for the tax. Selling property to raise cash to pay for the gift tax might not be cost effective. Having the donee pay the tax avoids the problem.

• Selling off appreciated property to pay a gift tax could generate an income tax liability.

Just as the reasons for wanting to make net gifts can be complicated, so are the reasons why a potential donee may agree to pay the gift tax. Here are some motivations for a potential donee to accept the gift tax liability.

• Owning specific property may be highly desirable now rather than later. For example, land you owned may lie alongside other land owned by a likely heir. If the donee could gain title to the land now, he or she could structure a deal to develop the total property. Waiting for a distribution from an estate could delay or derail the deal.

• Specific property included in an estate might not go to the person who most desires it. Paying the gift tax in order to gain immediate title to property would compensate for the uncertainty.

• A potential donee may agree to pay the gift tax on property that the donor would otherwise give to a charity. In either case the gross value of the estate is reduced by the value of the gift.

Net gifts can be complicated, involve little known income tax liabilities, and may offer limited benefits to either donor or donee. Approach this concept with caution and ask for legal help before proceeding.

Charitable Gifts

Gifts to acceptable charities can also reduce the size of your taxable estate. Charitable gifts enjoy two advantages over other types of gifts.

First, no limit applies to charitable gifts from estates after your death. Gifts to charities are deductible from income tax liabilities only up to 50 percent of your adjusted gross income each year during your lifetime.

Other limitations may apply to gifts of appreciated property that affect capital gains. Thus, bequests to be fulfilled after death are less restricted.

Second, gifts to charities can be set up in your will or living trust to take effect after your death. Thus, if you wish, you can always change the recipients or amounts noted in your will or living trust during your lifetime. The way your will or living trust reads at your death, when it becomes irrevocable, controls the disposition of your assets.

Direct gifts to a charity will qualify for deductions whether made while you are living or after your death. You must make sure that the recipient organization is qualified by the IRS as an acceptable charity. To qualify as an acceptable charity, the organization must be operated exclusively for religious, charitable, scientific, literary, or educational purposes. Furthermore, no part of its spending may benefit any individual. No substantial part of its activities may be engaged in propaganda or lobbying to influence legislation. Charitable organizations may not discriminate in their use of funds for reasons of religion, race, sex, age, or national origin.

Sometimes, contributions or interests in real property given to charitable organizations, to the federal government, or to a state or local government unit may be deductible from an estate even if they are not deductible on an income tax return. Direct bequests are limited to governmental units or charitable organizations within the United States. To leave assets to a charitable organization outside the United States, the bequest must be to a trust for the benefit of a charitable organization. (See Chapter 6 for more on this point.)

Don't assume from the name of an organization that it qualifies as a charitable organization. To be sure the charity you plan to leave money is qualified, check Internal Revenue Service Publication 78, Cumulative List of Organizations. This list can be purchased from the IRS and is updated regularly. An organization that is acceptable when you first draft your will, for example, may be removed and become unacceptable before your will is probated or your living trust is settled. Set up a contingent bequest to avoid having the desired deduction set aside in the event the charity becomes disqualified.

Your state's laws affecting wills and trusts may include limitations on charitable gifts. Some states limit a charitable deduction to no more than half of an estate's value. Or, bequests for religious or charitable purposes may not be ruled valid unless they were part of your will or living trust longer than 30 days before death.

Charitable gifts are not deductible if you or your heirs get something in return. You can't give money to a hospital on condition that rooms and services be given to members of your family before the money is made available to others, for example. However, if the will or trust is carefully written, some benefits may accrue to family members from a charitable bequest. A legitimate educational trust may, for example, permit the benefiting institution to select a member of your family if he or she is qualified for admission but lacks financial means to attend. If a number of applicants meet all requirements, the trustee may be directed to give preference to applicants with the same surname as the creator. The rule appears to be that a trustee may give preference to family members but may not limit awards to family members. Similar limitations may apply to a trust set up for the benefit of the children of a company's employees. Court rulings define acceptable language for gifts that could benefit family members. Your attorney will have access to these cases if you plan such charitable gifts.

Conclusion

Gifts provide useful tools for tailoring a will or living trust to minimize estate taxes. A variety of annual or once-in-a-lifetime gifts permit you to distribute assets to a number of recipients during your lifetime or to charities after your death.

Your key to a strategy of using gifts to minimize taxes is the size of your estate. If your taxable estate appears likely to exceed exemption limits, consider gifts as a way of giving future heirs some of your assets now rather than through a will or living trust.

CHAPTER NINE

Insurance

KEY TERMS IN THIS CHAPTER

custodial care
term life insurance
cash-value insurance
incidents of ownership
assigning ownership
three-year pull-back

group life insurance
lump-sum payment
annuity
settlements
affinity group
tax deferred annuity

Controlling risk and keeping possible losses within acceptable bounds remains the objective of varied insurance programs. Life, health, accident, and casualty (auto and home) coverage have long been the mainstays of prudent insurance programs during our lifetime. But estate planning calls for a different outlook on insurance coverage and the naming of beneficiaries for policies. Also, long term **custodial care** (nursing home) insurance affects older people and how they manage their assets.

Life Insurance

Life insurance has generally had two basic objectives. The first objective is to pro-tect dependents, particularly children, in case the primary breadwinner dies. Money paid to the beneficiary by the insurance company is intended to pay for the support that the decedent can no longer provide. Equally important is life insurance to provide for the support of children of a single parent. You may choose to play the odds, but the chance remains that one parent or other may die or be killed early in life. No matter how young you are, if you have a family, you should have a life insurance policy. In fact, when minor children are involved, estate planning relies heavily on insurance because the young family has had little time or opportunity to acquire assets.

The second objective is to provide a quick source of cash to pay for the expenses of settling an estate and to pay taxes, if any. Especially before the massive revision of estate tax law in 1976 when exemptions were very low, there was a need for ready cash to pay high estate taxes. Without the ready cash provided by insurance death benefits, the executor was forced to sell other assets, often at a fraction of their true value.

With the boost to an exemption on $600,000 per person, the number of estates whose taxable assets exceeded the limit declined markedly. In addition, the amount of taxes declined on estates that were required to file estate tax returns. In today's environment, continuing inflation and the remarkable growth of assets by many senior citizens are once again leading to a need for cash in the settlement of estates. Life insurance can meet that need, but it is not the only source of ready cash.

Ask yourself—"Do I really need life insurance?" Until recently many would have considered such a question absurd or irresponsible. Doesn't everyone needs insurance? Maybe we all need some kinds of insurance, but not everyone needs or should buy life insurance. A young man or woman who is self-supporting with no dependents has little need for life insurance. No one depends on him or her for financial support. If that person should die in an automobile accident, no one is likely to suffer a devastating financial loss. And with a limited time for that person to acquire assets, there would be no need for cash to settle an estate. Thus, neither of the usual needs for life insurance exists for young single people. When they marry and start having children, or if they have aging parents who will need

care, or if their assets expand beyond estate limits, then they need to consider life insurance needs.

The need for life insurance to protect children or other dependents is different from the need for cash in the estate of an elderly person. A two-stage plan can solve both needs or a single program may provide protection during one's younger years and assist in estate planning. First let's look at the two types of life insurance policies available.

Term Life and Cash-Value Policies

There are two basic types of life insurance policies: term life and cash value. Low-cost annual renewable **term life** policies offer insurance only. Since the risk of dying (or mortality risk) increases as one gets older, premiums on term policies increase annually. At ages above 55 or 60 annual premiums become onerous and uneconomic. One insurance company offers $500,000 of coverage for a man or woman age 30 for only $600 per year. At age 55 the premium increases to $3,700 per year.

Cash-value policies combine insurance with some sort of savings plan. They come in a bewildering variety. Separating and comparing the costs and benefits can be complicated at best or next to impossible at worst. Cash-value policies are usually level premium policies, that is, the premium stays the same until the policy is cancelled or paid for in full—possibly at age 99, or in other words, almost never. During one's younger years, the percentage of the premium going to the insurance cost or mortality cost will be considerably less than the percentage going to mortality costs when one is older.

The insurance company sets aside and invests these savings to build a reserve to cover the cost of insurance when you are older. Cash-value, level-premium policies are more practical than term life if you expect to carry insurance into retirement and beyond to provide a supply of ready cash for settling estate taxes and expenses. If, however, your taxable estate is not likely to exceed the tax-exempt limit, then carrying insurance into one's later life may not be prudent financial planning because ready cash will not be needed to pay taxes. Other liquid assets will typically be sufficient to cover settlement costs other than estate taxes.

Generally, you are better off to separate these two functions—insurance and savings (capital acquisition). In this way you can manage both more effectively.

The Two-Stage Plan

The first stage of the two-stage program for protecting dependents involves buying term policies on the lives of both parents. Both parents may work and both incomes may be needed to support the family, so both need insurance. Even when one parent remains at home to care for children, that parent's life needs to be insured. The cost of hiring a surrogate caregiver can mount to staggering sums. U.S. Department of Agriculture studies indicate that the cost of raising one child from birth to age 18 totals well over $100,000. Another four or five years of college may easily boost the tab for one child to $150,000. *Money* magazine for July, 1990, boosted the potential financial outlay significantly to more than $750,000 for four children in a family. These figures take the children to age 22 and include costs for private schools and university.

Term insurance provides an instant estate if the policyholder dies or is killed in an accident. The younger the children, the more coverage you need because young children will remain dependent for longer periods. If you have aging parents or other people who depend on you, you need to figure how much insurance you should buy based on the expected needs of the specific persons affected. At the time when young dependents' needs are greatest, you can afford more term coverage because rates are low. If you elect to buy cash-value policies, you may not be able to afford as much coverage as you need during the critical period when dependents are young. The first stage of this plan also involves investing income to build asset reserves. Presumably, if you spend less on premiums for term policies compared to cash-value policies, you can invest more of your income to build asset reserves. If you don't, then the two-stage plan will fail.

The second stage begins around age 50 to 55 when the annual premiums may become a significant drain on income. At that point you should have acquired enough assets through saving and investing for 30 or more years to drop your insurance coverage altogether. Thus, the two-stage plan calls for lots of low-cost term coverage while you are young and a reliance on accumulated assets when you are older.

The Single-Stage Plan

The single-stage plan calls for use of cash-value life insurance from the start. During later years the premium remains level and the policy provides the cash needed to pay estate taxes and expenses. Cash-value policies may also be turned into annuity programs for supplemental income. Cash-value life insurance violates one cardinal rule of financial planning—combining two functions. In this case risk management through insurance is combined with a savings plan. A far better practice is to buy pure insurance to satisfy one need. Save to acquire capital and manage investments separately.

Insurance in Estate Planning

Life insurance planning continues for a lifetime. You may need little or no insurance early on before you acquire dependents. And you may need large amounts of cash if your assets exceed estate exemption limits. While you can adjust coverages from time to time, when you start your insurance program and the number of years you pay insurance premiums will affect your estate and your estate planning.

How you handle the insurance part of your estate affects how much cash you may pass on to heirs or to charities. If you own an insurance policy on your life at the time of your death, all of the death benefits from the policy flow into your gross estate. Death benefits will include the face amount of the policy plus any reinvested dividends and accumulated interest. If you have a question about the amount that might be payable to your estate, ask your insurance agent for that information. Even if death benefits from a policy you own are paid directly to a beneficiary, they become part of your gross estate; they do not, however, pass through probate.

Owning your own policy means that you usually pay the premiums from your own funds and retain certain rights, known as "**incidents of ownership**." These include the right to name or change the beneficiary, to borrow against the cash value of the policy, and to terminate the policy for any reason.

Assigning Policy Ownership

If you give or assign all rights to an insurance policy on your life to another person, the death benefits are not included in your gross estate. If you attempt to retain any of the incidents of ownership, including the right to change beneficiaries, the policy remains yours and the death benefits will be included in your gross estate. The person who owns the policy on your life will also pay the premiums. If you give the person who owns your policy the cash, and he or she writes a check on his account to pay the premium, that qualifies as one part of being the owner. Or you may simply write a check on your own account to the policy owner. The beneficiary/owner endorses the check over to the insurance company to pay the premium.

As long as the annual premium dollar amount does not exceed the $10,000 annual gift limit, no gift tax is due and no gift tax return is required. If you attempt to give an existing policy with a cash value exceeding the $10,000 annual gift limit to a child or other person, be aware that gifts of insurance policies will be pulled back into your estate if you should die before three years have elapsed after assigning the policy. If you start a new policy, no cash value exists at the outset, so there is no gift over the $10,000 annual limit. Remember, however, that your age will affect the level of annual premiums. If you wait until you are into your forties or fifties, a cash-value policy could be expensive.

Assigning ownership of a life insurance policy on your life to another person, possibly a beneficiary, may be unnecessary as a tax-saving device. If your total estate will not exceed the $600,000 per person limit, allowing the death benefits from an insurance policy to fall into your estate will not matter.

Life Insurance Trust

When you transfer any asset to an irrevocable trust, you cannot reverse the process. Assigning a life insurance policy to an irrevocable insurance trust will remove the death benefits from your gross estate regardless of who the beneficiary is. Insurance policies that are candidates for inclusion in an irrevocable trust are term or group policies that have little cash value to you as long as you continue living. There is no cash value, for example, to be borrowed or regained on a termination of the policy. Thus, you are actually giving up nothing when you assign these policies to the trust. Your estate will benefit by not having to include the death benefits within the gross tabulation of assets. If you should assign a cash value policy to a trust, the **three-year pull-back** rule applies. If you should die before three years have elapsed, the cash-value policy reverts to the estate.

When establishing an insurance trust, be wary of the "incidents of ownership" rules. Suppose you name your spouse to be the trustee and beneficiary of the irrevocable insurance trust. Managing the trust is one of the incidents of ownership; thus, the spouse could be considered the owner and the assets of the trust would fall into his or her estate. A way to avoid this would be to structure an insurance trust so that it pays only the income from the investment of death benefits that are under the direction of a trustee other than your spouse. The principal would go to another beneficiary when your spouse dies. Not having any of the incidents of ownership keeps the death benefits out of the surviving spouse's estate.

Group Insurance

Many companies provide **group life insurance** coverage on their employees' lives as a fringe benefit. The federal government permits a company to charge off the cost of the employee life coverage as an expense. But the employee need not include the value of the life coverage in his or her income as long as death benefits do not exceed $50,000. Beyond that limit the annual cost of the excess coverage is considered added compensation and is subject to income tax. Generally, paying for excess coverage is not an economical way to buy more life insurance. If you should be rated uninsurable for an individual policy, however, you might acquire additional group coverage by paying for it. Group insurance is almost invariably term coverage. (Some exotic split dollar policies (combinations of term and cash value insurance) are sometimes available, particularly to the owners of small businesses. These policies are outside this discussion; if you are interested, ask a local insurance salesperson.)

Your company may also carry some form of accident and/or health insurance, often to cover the hazards of travel or on-the-job risks. Amounts payable from accident or health policies offered as a fringe benefit by your employer are not subject to the $50,000 limit on straight group life coverage.

Keeping death benefits payable on company group or accident/health policies out of your estate calls for advance planning. You may assign ownership rights to a beneficiary or to an insurance trust. The IRS at one point challenged the assignment of company paid group life policies to beneficiaries on the basis that the employee retained an incident of ownership: He or she could, the IRS reasoned, terminate the policy by quitting or getting fired. This question was resolved and group life insurance policies may now be assigned to a beneficiary or to a trust for the purpose of removing death benefits from the employee's estate.

The three-year pull-back rule remains. If you assign your rights in a group policy to a beneficiary and die before three years, the death benefits will fall back into your estate. While this rule seldom leads to problems, you should monitor the insurance company that provides the policies. If your company changes insurance carriers, the three-year clock might start again. You may be able to avoid this problem if your assignment of ownership includes a reference to any new carriers that may be used by the company in the future. Be sure that your assignment retains none of the incidents of ownership.

Settlement Options

When a beneficiary receives death benefits directly from the insurance company or through an estate, a number of options are available for how the money is to be paid. As the owner of the policy you may specify how the death benefits are to be received or you may allow the beneficiary to choose. The various options include, but are not limited to the following.

Lump-sum payment. The beneficiary may elect to receive all of the death benefits at one time. Because the premiums used to pay for the policy came from after-tax earnings by the owner and the buildup of cash value within policy accrues tax free, all death benefits are free of taxes to the beneficiary. At one time as many as 94 percent of the beneficiaries elected to receive all death benefits in a lump sum. Investing the **lump sum payment** may provide more income

than taking payments directly from the insurance company. Still, this option should be approached with caution by the policy owner. Be sure you know the money-managing ability of your beneficiary before agreeing to a lump sum payment.

Annuity. Under this option, the beneficiary may receive a fixed number of dollars each month over his or her lifetime. At the death of the beneficiary after any number of years, the insurance company retains any dollars that are left; no residual remains for heirs. This one-life contract can be modified with various stipulations that the **annuity** payments are to continue for some specific period—say ten years. If the beneficiary dies before that period ends, his or her heir continues to receive the annuity payments through the end of the stipulated period. Another option also allows an annuity to continue for a specific period, but if the annuitant dies before the end of the period, the money remaining in the account is paid to the annuitant's heir in a lump sum. Selecting the single-life period provides the maximum dollar annuity. When an insurance company agrees to pay monthly amounts over at least ten years, the monthly annuity will be less than the life contract. Periods may be ten, fifteen, twenty years, or some other time frame. Whatever the period, once it ends, nothing remains. If an annuitant selects the single life period and dies after three months, the insurance company retains the remainder.

Installment payments over a fixed period. This option differs from the common annuity because the time period is limited whether the beneficiary is alive or not. The amount of the income obviously varies according to the death benefits accumulated at the decedent's death, rate of interest earned by the principal that remains with the insurance company, and the period over which installments are to be paid.

Interest only. Requiring the insurance company to pay only the interest on the retained death benefits may be the option of choice when the owner believes the beneficiary may squander the cash. This option is much like a mini-spendthrift trust. At the death of the beneficiary, the principal retained by the insurance company is paid to the beneficiary's heirs.

Settlements, that is, the payout of death benefits from life insurance policies, are protected from creditors. Only the Internal Revenue Service can attach funds retained by an insurance company for the benefit of a beneficiary at the death of the policy owner.

Survivor Tax-Paying Insurance

Consider the possibility that the taxable estate you and your spouse accumulate exceeds the $1.2 million exemption level. One option is to defer the taxes on any excess property in your estate until the death of your spouse. Estate taxes would then be due on all property in the taxable estate of the surviving spouse in excess of the $600,000 exemption. You can now buy a joint and last survivor life insurance policy designed specifically to pay taxes due on the surviving spouse's estate. Depending on your age and the age of your spouse, joint and last survivor life insurance can be quite reasonable. When two lives are insured jointly with payments due after the second death, premiums can be lower than if single policies were to be issued on the life of each spouse, barring a great disparity in their ages. In fact, if it is handled right, earnings from estate assets passed along to the sur-

viving spouse may pay the premiums for the survivor policy.

Death benefits paid by the joint and last survivor policy would be available to pay taxes on property in excess of the $600,000 exemption limit following the surviving spouse's death. Obviously, the face amount of the policy needs to be determined from the size of the estate.

Increasing Insurance Coverage

While planning your estate, you may find your insurance is inadequate to pay taxes or expenses, or to leave enough assets to support your spouse. If you had managed your money more effectively during the earlier periods of your life, you might not find yourself in this predicament. But now, late in life, you decide you need more insurance. What can you do?

Two problems immediately arise:

1. Buying insurance late in life can be expensive. Mortality tables project life expectancies. If you are already well along in years, your life expectancy may be limited. Insurance companies figure their risks on the basis of mortality tables and set premium levels accordingly. If you are insurable, buying term coverage will continue to be your best alternative.

2. You may be uninsurable; that is, your general health or recognizable physical problems may preclude buying insurance at any price. An insurance company may consider you to be an unacceptable risk. A previous heart attack, a risky lifestyle that includes smoking or drinking, or a disease, such as diabetes, may limit your life expectancy. Insurance companies avoid accepting known losses, so you can't buy private individual insurance. There are alternatives, but they tend to be expensive.

Group insurance may still be available to you. Here are some options that may be open to you.

Credit life insurance is offered by mortgage lenders. A form of declining term can be relatively cheap when purchased from the lender who holds your mortgage loan. Declining term policies pay a smaller death benefit each succeeding year until the end, when no benefit is paid. Insurance may be written to cover the remaining loan principal. If you die before the principal is paid off, the insurance policy will pay the loan balance. The declining term policy covers successively smaller amounts each year to match the declining principal amount of the loan. Death benefits are assigned to the lender and a contingent beneficiary may receive any excess. While your estate or beneficiary does not receive a large sum, other assets will be freed from paying off the mortgage loan. Mortgage insurance thus increases your insurance coverage.

If you have owned your house for a number of years and the principal is nearly paid off, mortgage insurance may not be available. Policies are usually limited to the amount of the outstanding principal when you buy coverage. If you desperately need more insurance and have no other option, you could refinance your house loan to increase the principal amount that could be insured. Investing the proceeds of the loan would help to pay the loan interest and the insurance premium.

Credit cards offered by VISA, MasterCard, and others offer insurance to cover unpaid balances. These policies are mainly for the banks' benefit. They use the proceeds from the credit policies at your death to pay off loan balances to avoid the delays and hassles of collecting from an estate. The lender is the prime beneficiary, not you. Credit card insurance coverage tends to be expensive. If you are eligible, covering unpaid balances as a part of your overall insurance program will serve you better than buying separate credit card insurance coverage. But if you are not insurable, credit insurance could add a minor bit of protection.

Affinity groups may provide limited amounts of group coverage in the range of $10,000 to $25,000 face amounts without a physical examination. You may belong to a business association, such as an association of public accountants, civil engineers, purchasing agents, or any of the other thousands of similar organizations that offers such coverage. If your need is desperate, join several organizations in order to participate in their group life insurance plans. The price will be quite reasonable.

Group insurance plans where you work usually include provisions for converting your term coverage to cash value insurance when you retire or quit. If your employer covers you for the tax-free limit of $50,000, you may be able to convert to an individual cash value policy. Group rates, however, will not apply to this policy, and the conversion privilege will seldom offer term insurance. You may be stuck with an expensive cash value policy for two reasons: First, you are most likely to convert your group insurance late in life, possibly at your retirement, when cash-value policy rates are high due to mortality risks. Second, because the conversion privilege is available without demonstrating insurability, the insurance company assumes you are converting because you are otherwise uninsurable. So the insurance company tacks on an extra premium to cover what it assumes to be an added risk. Even considering the added costs of converting group coverage to an individual cash value policy, such a plan offers one way to increase your insurance coverage.

Tax Deferred Annuities

Changes in the tax laws have provided insurance companies with the incentive to offer a variety of investment programs designed to exploit certain tax code loopholes. The tax-free buildup of cash values under the protective umbrella of life insurance is one instance of such a program. The saving portion of life insurance premiums forms a cash pool for investing by the life insurance company. They may buy real estate, bonds, or stocks to develop a varied portfolio. When you own a cash-value life insurance policy, you own a proportionate share of those holdings. Further, income from the investments accumulates tax free unless you convert it to an annuity or cancel the policy and take out the cash value. At that point you will be taxed on the income over your initial investment. Death benefits paid to your beneficiary are free of income taxes, but they could impact your estate taxes.

By packaging investments with life coverage, insurance companies can offer attractive investment opportunities. Two of the many different programs are described below.

Tax deferred annuities (TDA) permit you to invest cash in a package that may guarantee a fixed rate of interest on your balance. A small amount of insurance will be packaged with the investment to permit deferment of any taxes until you withdraw earnings or principal. Premiums for the insurance will be subtracted from the gross yield. Substantial costs may be associated with the TDA, particularly if you attempt to withdraw funds before some minimum number of years, say ten, have elapsed. Since your original investment comes from after-tax money, tax benefits accrue only after your money is invested in the TDA. If the TDA ends up in your estate following your death, either limited or no taxes will be due on the buildup of asset value.

Single-premium life insurance policies come in two flavors: single-premium whole life (SPWL) or single-premium variable life (SPVL). In both cases earnings from the invested cash value compound tax free. Policies include a small life insurance death benefit that may or may not require a physical examination. Small dollar amount policies may not require a physical exam, while very large policies undoubtedly will. Each insurance company sets its own rules.

Under an SPWL policy, the insurance company guarantees to pay a specified interest rate for a minimum number of years, typically five. After that the rate may change, but it will normally be at or higher than some floor, typically $3\frac{1}{2}$ to 5 percent. Under the SPVL policy, your money may be invested in equity (stock), bonds or money market mutual funds. Returns will vary according to the performance of the mutual fund(s), and you may switch the proportions of your money between the three options from time to time.

Both types of single-premium life policies are designed to pass through to your estate. They offer an opportunity to increase the cash portion of your estate assets because the earnings from your assets compound tax free. You avoid payment of income taxes annually on these earnings, so the portion that would otherwise be taxed accumulates in your estate. The total death benefits pass to beneficiaries without being taxed, unless your taxable estate exceeds the exemption limit.

Investing your money in a SPWL or SPVL policy doesn't mean you no longer have access to the money. These policies usually offer no-cost or low-cost loans against the value of the policies. You may ordinarily borrow any of the earnings at no cost; that is, you pay no interest on those policy loans. If you borrow portions of your original capital, a typical interest rate is 2 percent of the loan amount.

Severe penalties aim to discourage cancelling the policy. First, you may be charged a surrender fee as high as 9 percent of the balance in the account. Further, you will be taxed on all policy earnings and any loans you may have taken. A different earnings figure may apply if you cash out the policy than if it remains in force until your death. Administrative fees charged by the insurance company may range from 2 to 3 percent. The investment is relatively secure, depending on the financial stability of the insurance company. Returns tend to be lackluster with the whole life policies returning average bond rates and variable policies tending to lag behind average mutual fund performance. Investing in a single-premium life policy could provide more cash among the assets of your taxable estate.

Long-Term Care Insurance

People are living longer, as medical science invents new drugs and devices to prolong life. But often those years are ones of declining physical and mental ability, perhaps to the point where one can no longer care for oneself. An older person may be bedridden or unable to move about, except in a wheelchair. He or she may spend months or years in a nursing home receiving custodial care.

Medicare, the government's great provider of hospital and medical care, does not cover the cost of custodial care. At $2,000 to $3,500 per month, such care can devastate one's assets and deplete a future estate. Congress passed a Medicare Catastrophic Coverage Act in 1988 to be financed by taxes on persons eligible for Medicare benefits, but the hue and cry was so loud and bitter that Congress recalled the act. Individuals remain responsible for their own care unless they use up all but a minimum level of savings. Then, the patient can receive custodial care paid for by Medicaid, a state program.

Here is an example of how depleted a couple's assets can become.

Marge and Orrin K. were in their late seventies, living frugally in a small house they had owned for over 40 years. Orrin, four years older than his wife, slipped and broke a hip while taking out the rubbish. Surgery to reconstruct the hip was complicated by bone structure weakened by osteoporosis. He was never able to walk again and could move about in a wheelchair for only short periods because he could not sit comfortably.

Marge tried valiantly to care for him in their home, but she was not strong enough to move him about. The only solution was a nursing home. The couple's savings totaled $86,000 and, in addition, they owned their house free and clear. The nursing home cost $2,000 per month. Her Social Security benefits were $470 per month, and she could earn about $500/month working part-time after Orrin was moved into the nursing home. They lived in a community property state. Their savings began to evaporate, and Marge applied for state aid through Medicaid. Conditions were stringent. Medicaid would not pick up the tab until her assets were no more than $2,000 plus certain exempt assets, including the house and their old car. All of the couple's assets were considered, as they were community property. Marge looked into giving some of their savings to their son, but only assets transferred 30 months earlier were exempt. Any transfer within the 30-month period had to be spent to support Orrin. She could keep up to $1,500 per month for herself, including the SS benefits.

Orrin never left the nursing home. Costs mounted and after nearly three years, the couple's assets were depleted to the exempt level of $2,000. Medicaid then picked up the cost of maintaining him in a nursing home, but he had to move to a cheaper home because Medicaid did not cover the higher cost of the first one. The new location was far removed from their home, and Marge began having trouble driving their old car. A son in the area would drive her two or three days a week, but she had been visiting Orrin daily.

When Orrin died over five years after entering the first nursing home, Marge was practically penniless. She sold their house and moved into a tiny apartment where she lived on a sparse income with some help from her children, something she had dreaded from the start.

If you believe there must be a better way, there is. It's called "Long-Term Care Insurance."

Numerous insurance companies now offer these policies for paying the cost of custodial care for a person in a nursing home. Different companies cite various statistics on the need. Generally, you can figure you have roughly one chance in four of ending up in a nursing home at some time in your life. Your stay may be only a few weeks, or it could be years. Only six percent of persons survive in a nursing home for longer than four years. Advantages cited by insurance companies in their pitch for nursing home insurance include:

• Custodial care is expensive, running as high as $50,000 per year. Many couples cannot afford such a cash outflow without selling their home or other assets to raise cash.

• Choices may be extremely limited among nursing homes that accept Medicaid. States are notoriously stingy with payments, and homes cut costs where they can, sometimes to the perceived detriment of patients.

• Carrying nursing home insurance permits you to spend your assets without worry. Many people keep large amounts of cash available thinking they may need custodial care at some time in the future. They do not enjoy the comforts and joys of retirement because of the overhanging fear of having to pay for long term care. Custodial care insurance is a backup that allows them to spend more freely than they would without an alternative source of funds.

• Adult children may fear that they will be called upon to aid their aging parents financially. To avoid nursing homes paid for by Medicaid, children may chip in and buy nursing home insurance for one or both parents.

There are disadvantages to this type of insurance: Long-term care policies are expensive. Rates vary according to a number of variables—age, pre-existing conditions, number of years covered, benefit levels, inflation protection, and company policies. You may choose the benefit level you want. For an added premium the benefit value you select will be increased yearly to compensate for inflation. A typical inflation rate is 4 percent per year. Many persons choose some figure less than the projected full cost. They prefer to assume part of the risk to reduce the premium. Typically, insurance companies offer policies that may run for three, four, or five years. A few companies offer lifetime care; as long as you must remain in a nursing home, benefits continue. Pre-existing conditions may not be covered for six months to a year, although some policies pay for care from day one.

The Catastrophic Care Program passed by Congress raised such an uproar that it was repealed. Some senior citizen groups continue to lobby for a program that would pay for both catastrophic medical expenses and nursing home care. The previous program omitted nursing home coverage.

When shopping for a custodial care policy, consider the following:

• Does coverage begin with the first day of your admission to a nursing care facility, and is admission direct? Avoid policies that require some minimum stay in a hospital or skilled care facility before qualifying for admission to the nursing home.

• Are there limitations due to pre-existing conditions? Any limitations must be clearly spelled out.

• Is care for Alzheimer's disease included for as long as the policy remains in force?

• Will premiums cease for some period of confinement in a home?

• Do benefits rise regularly to offset inflation with no increase in premium?

Premiums are becoming more competitive as insurance firms gain experience and more companies enter the field. Companies that pioneered in this field approached the concept of long-term care insurance reluctantly and with many misgivings due to a lack of definitive cost data. As they became more experienced, large premiums designed to cover the unknowns were dropped.

Shop for coverage by asking for proposals from several companies to compare benefits and costs. No one policy serves everyone best.

Conclusion

Insurance can provide cash benefits to care for dependents early in life or provide cash to pay estate taxes and expenses following your death. How you buy insurance and how you plan your estate can influence the amount of insurance you need. Who owns the policies affects the size of your taxable estate. Keeping death benefits out of your estate may provide a tax advantage if your estate is at or over the exemption level.

Nursing home insurance may affect your estate directly and protect your bequests to beneficiaries. It is an alternative worth considering.

Community Property

Nine states, mainly in the western part of the United States, consider spouses as equal owners of property acquired by either or both during the marriage. This is known as community property with the marriage being the community. The concept of community property may be traced back as far as the Visigoths of Europe in the second century. It was passed on to the western areas of the United States via Spanish explorers. Eight states, California, Washington, Arizona, Idaho, Texas, Nevada, New Mexico, and Louisiana have operated under community property laws since they were admitted to the union, although most of them have changed portions of the law from time to time. Wisconsin recently joined the list of states with essentially the same philosophy but with different wording of the statutes. History has it that men and women worked hard and shared hardships together in settling the frontiers. In light of this,

women insisted that they were equal partners and deserved an equal share in any property value created by the community; that is, the married couple.

Even under the community property umbrella, some states permit more control over the assets by the husband than by the wife when both spouses are living. The other 41 states and the District of Columbia function as **common law** states. Community property at the death of one spouse is divided differently than in common law states. Property owned by couples in common law states may belong to the person who contributed the money to acquire it. Or, property is assumed to belong to the man regardless of who paid for it. Conditions vary widely according to how the common law developed. When considering estate planning options, you must clearly understand the differences between community, or marital, property and separate property.

The following discussion of the property rights of couples living in nine community property states applies only to married couples. Unmarried couples living together do not own community property. If you are one of an unmarried couple and choose to own property jointly, you owe it to yourselves to develop an agreement that clearly spells out your rights and obligations. Laws and procedures developed over many years for married couples, widows and widowers, will not protect you if you are not married.

What Is Community Property?

Basically, all property including real estate, investments, personal property, and cash or cash equivalents acquired by a married couple during their marriage is community property in the nine community property states. Each spouse holds an equal share in the property regardless of who paid for it, how it was acquired, or how it is used. The federal Uniform Marriage and Divorce Act (UMDA) is an attempt to bring the various state laws dealing with ownership of property and the division of property in divorces into conformance. The UMDA has been helpful in revising the laws in 38 states over the past 16 years to minimize differences. Section 307(c) of the UMDA defines marital property as "all property acquired by either spouse subsequent to the marriage and prior to a decree of legal separation is presumed to be marital property regardless of whether title is held individually or by the spouses in some form of co-ownership such as joint tenancy, tenancy in common, tenancy by the entirety and community property." In community property states property acquired after marriage is owned equally by the two spouses except when it meets the rules of separate property.

Separate Property

Separate property is owned by one spouse; ownership is not shared with the other spouse. The difference between what is marital or community property and what is separate property hinges on how and when the property was acquired. Separate property may be any of the following:

• *Any and all property owned by either spouse prior to marriage*. How this separate property is managed after marriage will determine how long the property originally owned by each spouse remains separate. When widows, widowers, or divorcees marry late in life, a **prenuptial agreement**, that is, a contract agreed to by the couple before marriage, may list and define each person's separate property and their intention to keep it separate from the community. Provisions in a prenuptial agreement can preserve property to be distributed to the children of each spouse or to avoid a messy dissolution if the marriage doesn't work out.

• *All property given to one spouse or inherited by one spouse regardless of how long the couple was married*. Rules vary from state to state regarding the income from inherited or gifted property after it is received by one or the other spouse as separate property. A few states, such as California and Washington, permit the income earned from separate property to remain as part of the separate property. In Texas any income earned from separate property becomes community property. Only the original gift or inheritance remains as separate property.

• *Property acquired after a permanent separation is classed as separate property*.

Segregating Separate Property

If you live in one of the community property states and wish to retain clear title to your separate property, you must take steps to keep it segregated from your community property. If you should acquire a piece of real estate and the title is in your name alone, you can keep it separate by retaining the title. If the property earns income, you may keep the income as your separate property except in Idaho and Texas. Suppose your real estate is an apartment house earning income from rentals. Your best approach is to consider the rental as a small business. Open a separate bank account for deposits of rent and as a source of cash for maintenance, taxes, insurance, and other expenses. Avoid, at all costs, any hint of **commingling** (mixing together). Net income from your separate property will be combined with your income from work or other community property investments and the income from your spouse, if any, when filing federal income tax returns. Filing a joint tax return does not infringe on your separate property rights.

You may retain stock, bonds, mutual fund shares, and similar investments in your name as separate property only as long as they meet the acquisition rules noted earlier. Even if you buy stock in only your name after marriage, the shares will be considered as community property if you bought shares with community funds. To be considered as separate property, you must have owned the shares prior to marriage or inherited them.

You may choose to convert separate property to community property informally or formally. If you casually commingle your property with that of your spouse, it will lose its identity. For example, suppose you receive a gift of $10,000 from your father. If you deposit the check in your joint account with your spouse, the money may no longer be identified as separate property. It has been hopelessly commingled with money that is clearly community property.

When people marry, they may own various kinds of personal property, such as a car, sports equipment, clothing, jewelry, and investments. As time passes, the car wears out and is replaced, clothes are tossed out and replaced with new pieces, and other property may be used and replaced. What was once easily identifiable as separate property becomes commingled and is no longer separate property.

You may formally convert your separate property to community property by ignoring its status or by declaring the change in writing. If you own a house with the title in your name when you marry, it may be converted to community property by changing and recording the title to show both spouses as joint owners. For real estate the change must be in writing. In some community property states one spouse may give his or her share of ownership in the marriage community's property to the other spouse. Such gifts must usually be formalized in writing.

If you formerly served in one of the military services and are in line for a pension, that pension will be considered equally owned by both spouses in community property states. Divisions of private pensions may hinge on how long the couple has been married at the time of the first death and the proportion of income contributed. Neither Social Security nor Railroad Retirement pensions may be lumped together as community property. Federal law mandates them to be separate property according to who earned the credits.

When separate property appreciates, what happens to the differential value in the event of, say, a divorce? If you owned the property, for example, real estate or investments, as separate property before marriage or if you inherited the property, you will most probably retain all of the appreciation. You must follow the steps outlined earlier about keeping the property segregated, including any income. However, if you own a rental house as separate property, for example, and spend community funds to maintain it, you may have to share some or all of the appreciation depending on what percentage of the appreciated value might have resulted from the money spent on maintenance. To avoid possible problems during a divorce or an estate division, either keep the property completely separate or convert it to community property.

Community Property Agreements

Planning for the distribution of your assets will differ if you live in one of the nine community property states than if your state is governed by common law property statutes. Since each spouse owns an equal share in the property, each half must be considered separately. The simplest way to convey property to your spouse at your death is with a **community property agreement**. This simple, one-page contract contains three provisions:

1. All of the couple's property is community property. None of their property is separate property.

2. All property to be acquired in the future by either of the spouses will also be community property.

3. When either spouse dies, the survivor owns all of the community property.

For small estates, the community property agreement, when filed with the recorder of deeds or a similar department of county government, satisfies all legal requirements regarding dispersal of the estate. Everything that was previously owned by the two spouses now belongs to the surviving spouse—no will to be probated and no trusts to take effect after death.

Obviously, the simple community property agreement will not do the job if one or other of the spouses owns separate property, if the couple's estate valuation exceeds the $600,000 exemption level at either the first or second death, or if special provisions for gifts to charity or dependent persons necessitate creating a trust. While a community property agreement may simplify requirements for transferring title to a surviving spouse, it cannot be used when the surviving spouse dies. At that time the estate must go through probate unless a living trust is in effect. You cannot rely on a community property agreement as your sole estate plan.

Drawbacks of Community Property Agreements

Community property agreements can also lead to legal complications when the persons involved do not look ahead to possible changes in their situation, as happened in the two following cases.

Edna and Boris K. signed a community property agreement nearly 10 years before Boris died. At the time the couple signed the agreement and at the time of Boris' death, the couple's taxable estate was just over $400,000. Before the agreement was signed, however, Boris and his brother Alex received title to a piece of unimproved land from their father. The brothers owned the property as joint tenants with right of survival (the surviving joint tenant of the property owns the property outright). Following Boris' death Alex claimed clear title to the property that had been given to him and Boris jointly. Edna, however, claimed a half interest in the property because the community property agreement gave her all of the couple's property. Both claims had some legitimacy. The case was appealed to the state supreme court.

Finally, both Alex and Edna were awarded equal but undivided interests in the property as "tenants in common." Neither could sell his or her half of the property without the approval of the other. They could also bring suit to have the property equitably divided.

Certainly, this was not the result intended by the father who gave the property to his two sons.

Here's another example of how a community property agreement might result in some unforseen—and undesirable—circumstances.

Late in the 1970s, Fred and Charlene S. married, both for the second time. Fred owned only minimal personal property with no investments or real estate. Charlene, a widow, owned nearly half a million dollars of stock and bonds plus a house whose mortgage was paid off. She brushed aside the suggestion that she should prepare a prenuptial agreement and keep her property separate after the marriage. Instead, she signed a community property agreement that converted all of her property to community property.

After 14 years of marriage, Fred sought a divorce. As is the custom, all of the community property was divided equally between the parties. Charlene disagreed, claiming that Fred's petition for dissolution of the marriage effectively nullified the community property agreement. Instead of an even split, she argued that she should be given the bulk of their community property because she had contributed most of it. There had been little value added during the 14 years of marriage. Again the case was appealed and the Court of Appeals rejected Charlene's contention that the petition for divorce changed the previously signed community property agreement. The court said, in effect, that a contract existed and the divorce petition had no effect on it.

Different Ways of Looking at Community Property Agreements

Planning for the distribution of property owned by spouses in a community property state can go in several different directions to take care of specific needs not covered by a simple community property agreement. For example, if the taxable value of the estate exceeds $600,000 at either the first or second death, a tax-saving trust can save important estate tax dollars. Assets placed in the tax-saving trust no longer remain in the estate of the surviving spouse, although he or she gets all of the income from the assets in the trust and may invade the principal under certain conditions.

Suppose the community of Mary and John Doe own assets that total $900,000 after paying expenses and settlement costs. Neither spouse owns separate property. If John dies first, his half of the community property goes into an irrevocable trust, and Mary is the trustee of John's trust. She is entitled to income from the assets in the trust but does not own the assets. They remain in trust for the couple's children at Mary's death.

Because John's half of the couple's community property totals less than the $600,000 exemption level, there is no estate tax liability. A testamentary trust that would go into effect as a part of the probate of John's will would accomplish the same end result. At Mary's death her half of the couple's property totals $450,000. With John's property in trust for their children, it does not fall into Mary's estate. Again no estate tax would be due. If John's estate had been given without reservation to Mary either by provisions in a will, living trust, or community property agreement, Mary's taxable estate would have totaled $900,000. At her death her estate would have been liable for an estate tax of $114,000.

A similar saving of taxes occurs when the couple's assets exceed $1.2 million in value. A tax-saving trust uses the full exemption of $600,000 available to each spouse to minimize taxes. This arrangement is more fully explained in Chapters 4 and 5.

In most community property states a special provision favors the cost basis of a house owned as community property. Ordinarily, in a common law state the value of the house is divided equally. In some states, including New York, the first to die may be declared the owner and the house is awarded a total stepped-up value. If the half that belonged to the decedent receives a stepped-up value equal to half of the market value of the house and the surviving spouse later sells the house, any capital gains or losses must be figured on two halves of the property (see the table on page 141.) In most community property states both halves of the house value are stepped up to the market value. Any capital gains or losses from a subsequent sale are figured from the single stepped-up cost basis for the entire house.

Distributing Separate Property

When one or both spouses own separate property, its distribution cannot be handled with a community property agreement. A will or living trust is needed to specify how separate property will be distributed. If a husband dies first, his estate consists of half of the couple's community property plus all of his separately owned property. If the total of his half of the community property and all of his separate property totals more than the $600,000 exemption level, his estate may be subject to estate tax. If a tax-saving trust has been written into the husband's will or living trust, up to $600,000 may be exempted, including all or some of his separate property.

At the second death the surviving spouse's estate will be treated similarly with the exception that no tax-saving trust can be used. Her own estate includes her half of the original estate as it existed when the husband died plus any separate property of her own. If these properties total more than the $600,000 exemption, then her estate will be liable for estate taxes.

If one part of a married couple's property is a business owned originally by one spouse and maintained as separate property, special arrangements should be made to assure continued management outside of the family. A **buy-sell agreement** may provide a partner or co-owner the opportunity to buy the decedent's interest in the business at a predetermined price. If the value of the business falls into the decedent's estate as separate property, it may boost his or her estate's value over the exemption limit.

If the married couple own and work in the business together, the asset value of the business will be community property in

**TWO-STEP CALCULATIONS OF JOINTLY OWNED HOUSE WHERE ONE-HALF
RECEIVES STEPPED-UP VALUE AT FIRST DEATH***

Jointly owned house

Original cost basis	$50,000
Capital addition of bedroom	40,000
Cost basis at first death	$90,000
Estate value of house at first death	$310,000
Spouse A's stepped-up half	$155,000
Spouse B's cost basis after spouse A's death as survivor	$45,000
Spouse B sells house for (net)	$350,000
Spouse A's half of the taxable gain	$20,000
($175,000 – $155,000)	
Spouse B's half of the taxable gain	$130,000
($175,000 – $45,000)	
Total taxable gain**	$150,000

* Separation into two halves not effective in all states.
** $125,000 exemption from federal tax may apply if Spouse B is over age 55 and meets the three-of-past-five-years occupancy requirements.

those nine states. If the surviving spouse chooses not to continue operating the business, problems of valuation and selling can be complicated. If you find yourself in this position, seek professional advice early to avoid problems down the road.

Moving from State to State

You may now be living in a community property state. You have drafted a will or developed a living trust in response to your state's property laws. You decide to move to another state with common law property rights. Ordinarily, if you have a will or living trust, its provisions will be legal in all states. Problems may arise, however, with the separate property each spouse owns and which each may, thus, leave to different beneficiaries. Ownership of separate property is seldom a problem, as its ownership is well documented. Ownership of certain assets within the community of a married couple is something else. Each spouse technically owns half of the couple's community property, but dividing the property could mean one spouse ends up with real estate while the other holds cash. For example, the husband may buy a house in the new location using money from a lump sum paid out by his former employer. He may insist that the house is his and is no longer community property, as it would be if they lived in the former community property state. Further, the idea of all property being jointly owned may have rankled either or both spouses. When they move and are no longer bound by community property laws, they may decide to divide the property differently in a will or living trust. If you move from a community property state to a common law state, you're probably better served by writing a new will or living trust. If you and your spouse have any disagreements over dividing your property, straighten the problem out early, even if it means consulting an attorney.

Property rights when moving from a common law state to a community property state will depend on which state you move to. If you move to California or Idaho, either of these states may consider the property acquired while married in a prior state of residence as community property, much as it would be if you had acquired it while living in California or Idaho. Other community property states recognize the status of the property according to how it was acquired in the common law state. After a time, assets acquired in your new community property state would be commingled and equally owned as community property regardless of who paid for the property or earned the income.

If you move from a community property state to another community property state, from Washington to California for example, nothing changes. Your separate property in Washington remains separate property in California. Community property in Washington remains community property in California. The situation is similar when moving from a common law state to another common law state. This said, you may still be wise to have your will or living trust reviewed by a knowledgeable attorney within your new home state.

Conclusion

Living in one of the nine community property states imposes different conditions on the disposition of property at the first and second deaths of spouses. Property may be owned jointly within the property rights spelled out in community property states or separately. You need to know how the different classes of property are distributed at the death of either spouse.

If you move from a state with one set of property rules to a state with different property rules, you should investigate possible changes needed in your estate plan. You may need to restructure your will or living trust to fit within the property system of your new home. Better to learn of any differences while you can still do something about them.

Management of Your Estate

At your death your estate will end up in somebody's hands to be managed or settled. If you are depending on a will to distribute your assets, an executor will manage the unbundling of your life's work and distribute your accumulated assets. Being an executor calls for a variety of management and interpersonal skills. Your executor must have unquestioned integrity, scrupulous ethics, and at the same time understand money in all of its many ramifications, keep well organized records, and be sensitive to the emotional needs of surviving family members.

The trustee you appoint to manage your living trust must be similarly qualified. You may elect to do the job yourself during your lifetime. But at death your spouse, may step in and assume the responsibilities of a trustee if he or she is qualified. A **co-trustee** might be appointed to manage your estate with your surviving spouse as a team after your

death. After the death of your spouse, who has been acting as trustee or co-trustee, the successor trustee you have selected steps in to assume the responsibility.

You will also need to appoint a lawyer to work with your executor or trustee to work out all the legal details of settling your estate.

Unless you draft a valid will or develop a living trust during your lifetime, the probate court will appoint its own manager called an administrator. Often court appointed administrators are next of kin or other relative of the deceased. But you might not have picked the appointed administrator for the job. But if you have not taken steps to provide for the management of your estate at your death, then your heirs must take what the court gives them. Unfortunately, you will not be around to contest the appointment and your heirs will have little voice in the selection.

Picking an Executor

Picking a family member may be a good idea if the person has at least some of the skills needed. Your oldest son or daughter might serve if he or she can be counted on to be fair and efficient. Your surviving spouse could be a good choice for several reasons—he or she will know the family, your assets, and your unspoken wishes. Further, the surviving spouse will likely know or remember much of the information required to file tax return forms and other paperwork needed to close out the estate. If the surviving spouse does not have the necessary skills, then appointing a knowledgeable co-trustee could be one way to insure good management of your estate.

When considering who will manage your estate after your death, remember how big the job can be. The executor (executrix if a woman or a personal representative in some places) will need to spend hours and hours over a period of months and possibly years taking apart and distributing all that you have accumulated. Don't underestimate the difficulties your executor will encounter. A major problem may be to locate the beneficiaries if they have moved out of the area. Or, some of the property specified in the will can't be found. Then, the question is—was it sold and the will not changed or did some person simply remove it?

A short list of an executor's duties includes the following:

• *Collecting and inventorying all of the decedent's property or the paperwork evidencing ownership.* After identifying all of the property, the executor must put a value on it that will withstand the scrutiny of the heirs and the Internal Revenue Service.

• *Filing tax returns.* A federal estate tax return may be required even if no tax is due.

A state or inheritance tax return must be filed in some states. If taxes at any level are due, they must be paid from the estate's funds. Of course, the source of those funds will have been identified in the inventory of assets.

• *Distributing assets in accordance with provisions of your will or living trust.* If you have done your job right in preparing your living trust, all of your assets will have been transferred to it. Your trustee will have those records to start. If you were not totally diligent in transferring assets to the trust, some assets may have to go through probate—with or without a will.

• *Meeting with one or more attorneys and accountants numerous times during the process of winding up the decedent's affairs.* Often the estate of the first of a couple to die is easily settled. Most or all of the property may be left to the surviving spouse. Winding up the estate of the second to die becomes more complicated. Obviously, the more one prepares and the more information left to the executor or trustee, the simpler will be the process. And the simpler the process, the less all of it will cost.

If you decide one of the family cannot do the job you expect or if that person refuses to accept the responsibility, your next choice could be a bank trust department, an acceptable and trustworthy attorney, a trusted and knowledgeable friend, or a relative who is not a member of the immediate family and who will not benefit from any of the proceeds of the estate. Banks or trust companies have one overriding advantage: they or a legal successor will always be there. The staff person in the trust department of the bank who handles your estate may not be sensitive to your family's needs, but he or she will be experienced and will handle the myriad details professionally. On the other hand, bank executors have not always been known for their speed in settling an estate. You should, however, consider appointing a bank trust department as the executor if your estate includes a business or substantial interest in a business that must be appraised for value or sold. Special expertise is needed in these complicated deals to get the best prices for assets sold or to avoid an excessive evaluation for tax reporting.

If you pick a nonprofessional as executor, be sure he or she is willing to serve. The person you pick must commit a significant amount of time to complete the job. The executor or trustee will be paid, of course, but adequate time might not be available. Also, the executor may be held personally liable if too much cash is paid out to heirs who profess a need for an immediate handout and the estate ends up with too little cash to pay taxes later. If the person you pick to be executor should move away, you may need to choose again. Travel and long distance telephone calls can run up the cost of settling the estate.

Anticipating Problems

Going through the steps necessary to settle an estate while you are still around to answer questions can help your executor or trustee tremendously. Part of this preparation will be your Letter of Instructions (see Chapter 12). Take on the role of coach. You know what you want done and understand more of the details about the property in your estate than anyone else. Don't take that information to the grave with you. If you have the foresight to develop a detailed will, spend a bit more time to assure your instructions will be carried out as you planned.

Start with the various schedules in the federal estate tax return, Form 706. You may request the full package of forms and instructions by writing to the IRS office that services your area. You can locate the nearest office by consulting your last package of income tax forms, asking your tax advisor, or calling the IRS. The forms are free.

Much of the information required for the estate tax return is the same as you collected on the worksheets for calculating the size of your estate in Chapter 2. Note Schedule 2A-7 Real Estate, for example. It calls for a listing of the real estate you own and an appraisal of its value at the date of death. An alternate valuation may be elected, but for the dry run you are most concerned about listing all of the property in your estate. You are the one person best able to compile the necessary information. You can dig out receipts, correspondence, or past tax receipts and assessments from some cubbyhole or file that your prospective executor may not know about. Imagine the problems your executor will have trying to locate and include all of your property if you don't help. Once you start working through the various schedules, you will recognize the need to pull all of the information together.

If you drafted your will several years earlier, a dry run through the various schedules of Form 706 will highlight areas where data may no longer be up to date. For example, suppose you had decided to give money or property to a charity. You could check to see if the charity is still acceptable to the IRS as a recipient of tax-deductible contributions. If the organization has been disqualified for any of a number of reasons, your bequest will not be deductible. If your will sets up a trust to receive a portion of your estate for some purpose, check to make sure you have relinquished all incidents of ownership. Otherwise, the trust will not be valid and your intentions will be frustrated.

Going over these details with your prospective executor and the lawyer you have chosen to help him or her accomplishes two objectives:

First, the review acquaints your executor-to-be with the details of your will and opens an opportunity for you to explain your reasons for certain of its provisions. In the unlikely event that you have decided not to provide any of your estate's assets to a son or daughter, you will have included a specific statement to that effect in your will, so that the disinherited son or daughter cannot assert that you had simply forgotten. But talking over the reasons for your decision to cut a child out of your estate will provide background for the executor to defend his or her actions in carrying out the provisions of your will.

Second, you may be reminded of property you have acquired since you wrote your will, or you may have acquired property since you wrote the will and neglected to provide directions for disposing of it. If you decide to review portions of your will with your executor and the attorney, the attorney may point out changes in the law that could affect taxes or complicate trusts or charitable provisions. If you have not reviewed your will since 1988, you should do it with your attorney, as changes in the law may affect how taxes are to be calculated.

You might find the task of running through the settlement of your estate distasteful, time consuming, and disturbing. It may bring back memories of deals gone bad or of costly mistakes. It may remind you of your mortality. But stick with it. Your knowledge of all the details that will make up your estate can simplify the job you have asked your executor to undertake.

The equivalent of a dry run is almost inevitable if you depend on a living trust to protect your estate rather than a will. If you are the trustee of your living trust, you will be working with it often, managing your assets just as if they were in your name. At your death a successor trustee steps in and manages the trust. If your successor trustee is your spouse, reviewing provisions in the trust provides an opportunity to train him or her. Without such an awareness of the complexities of your assets, possibly including a business or major interest in a business, your spouse will not be able to manage the trust effectively after you have gone.

One of the most important tasks for a husband who has routinely handled most of the money matters for his family is to teach his wife how to manage financial **resources** effectively. It will be necessary for her day-to-day survival as well as for the effective care or your estate.

Probating Your Will

Few changes ordinarily occur at a first death, as the surviving spouse typically receives the property you both owned together. Some property may be distributed to designated heirs and some assets may be distributed to charities, possibly to avoid estate taxes. If the will includes a testamentary tax-saving trust, it will become irrevocable as part of the probate process. The assets assigned to the trust will be set aside to be managed by the trustee you select. Ordinarily, barring unusual circumstances, the trustee of the tax-saving trust will be the surviving spouse. Income from the trust flows to the survivor during his or her lifetime. At the second death assets in the trust are distributed to beneficiaries.

One of the first actions to be taken by the executor is to consult with your attorney, preferably the one who drew the will, who will outline the steps to follow. A first consideration is an appraisal of your assets' value. Moving quickly on this point is essential because their fair market value must be determined as of the day of the decedent's death or the **alternate date** (six months after death). Using it is optional, and the executor must decide which data affords more benefits to the estate. Real estate markets, particularly, can change over a period of weeks or months. A professional appraiser may be needed to determine the fair market value of your house and any other real estate you may have owned as separate property or together. Other property, such as one or more cars, home furnishings, jewelry, and all manner of personal property you and your spouse owned must be valued by whatever method is acceptable and can be defended if challenged by the IRS. Antiques, jewelry, silver flatware, and similar items of value should be appraised by a knowledgeable person, preferably one who is licensed for such activities.

Determining the value of stocks and mutual fund shares is easy; simply check their value at the close on the day of the decedent's death or the alternate date. Unless bonds are listed, you will need to check with a broker for their bid value on the day of death. Shares in a closely held business or interests in a limited or general partnership are more difficult to value. A market seldom exists for the shares of a small business. An appraiser or consultant may be needed to place a reasonable value on those assets.

An estate tax return, Form 706, will need to be filed if the gross value of the decedent's assets exceeds $600,000. Even if expenses and other deductions reduce the taxable estate value to less than $600,000 and no estate tax is due, you and/or your attorney or accountant will need to complete and file the return. As noted earlier, Form 706 requires the listing of property from which the liability for taxes can be figured. Ordinarily, the estate tax return must be filed within nine months of death.

Delays in filing the tax return may result from the probate process itself, collecting all bills to be paid by the estate, settling claims, and other activities. During this period, few bequests to beneficiaries will be paid out. Cash must be preserved to pay any taxes due from the estate. Also, claims, loans, and bills must be cleared up.

All of these activities proceed under the authority of the probate court in a **supervised procedure**. Less formal procedures may be used in small estates. (See Chapter 4.) Witnesses to the will may be called to affirm that the signature is valid and the will is true. The will presented will be the "last will and testament" of the decedent, and one of the court's determinations will be to assure no other later wills exist. The court will review all actions by the executor and others brought in to assist to make sure they comply with the will itself and with applicable state and federal laws. Long delays are typically a part of the system. The usual probate may extend well over a year. A study by the American Association of Retired Persons in three cities around the United States indicated an average of 467 days for the proceedings for all cases. The time for modest estates averaged 420 days. Providing a will shortens the period of probate.

As part of the probate proceedings the executor will present a plan for the distribution of assets, usually after filing the estate tax return. When the estate is large and an estate tax is paid, probate may be put on hold until the IRS indicates an acceptance of the Form 706. When the probate court approves the distribution of assets and the validity of trusts set up in the will, the executor closes out the estate.

All probate proceedings are presented in public court. Interested persons can obtain the details of a will and contest provisions, possibly on frivolous grounds. Whatever the reason, challenges to a will may delay closing an estate for years. A living trust functions out of the limelight and few are challenged.

When the probate court approves, titles to real estate and other titled property may be changed to reflect the new owners. The new real estate titles will be recorded and the probate court case cited as authority. Later searches of title will show a clear transfer of title to the new owner. The executor will send stock and bond certificates to the **transfer agent**, possibly through a broker, for a name change. Stocks and bonds may be sold only if a signature matches the name on the certificate. Thus, new certificates must be issued to the new owner(s). Along with certificates in the name of new owners, the executor will normally supply a certified listing of the cost bases as of the date of the decedent's death. Often the cost basis will represent a stepped-up value. This is the same stepped-up value used in calculating the total value of the assets in the estate.

When assets cannot be physically and evenly divided among two or more listed beneficiaries, the executor may have to sell the property and divide the cash. If your will provides clear directions regarding such division, the executor is bound to follow them. For example, you may own 100 shares of XYZ Corp. You could direct your executor to distribute to each of three beneficiaries 33 shares plus one-third of the cash

received from selling the single share. But selling a single share can be costly because of brokers' minimum fees. A better way would be to give one beneficiary 34 shares if you prefer to retain the stepped-up cost basis for shares that may have appreciated substantially during the time you held them. Some other division could retain the equality of distributions if you believe that to be essential. Otherwise, direct your executor to sell all shares and divide the cash three ways.

When all activities have been accomplished in accordance with the will, the estate tax form has been filed and accepted and assets distributed, your attorney will file a petition for closing. As you can see, administering a will is no easy task for an executor.

Administering a Living Trust

When a person who has established a living trust dies, a different series of actions takes place. The trustee you have appointed to administer your living trust assumes responsibility. At your death the revocable living trust becomes irrevocable. Your direction for distribution of the assets must be followed exactly.

The trustee's first step will be to calculate the value of your estate in preparation for filing a federal estate tax return, Form 706. Having placed all of your assets in a living trust simplifies the job. The trustee will need to update values to the date of your death and check if any property may not have been included in the living trust. If you have done your job and placed all but a minimum of your assets in your living trust, your trustee will have a relatively easy time of it. If you have forgotten or neglected to put some substantial assets into your living trust, the assets outside the trust must go through probate. A "pour-over" will, as noted in Chapter 5, can be probated to pour over any leftover assets into your trust.

Your successor trustee can act independently in accordance with the provisions of your living trust to disburse assets without the delays and costs of a public probate. Otherwise, the major steps of appraising your estate, filing an estate tax return, and disbursing assets is similar to the actions of an executor.

Paying Estate Taxes

If the completion of an estate tax return, Form 706, calls for the payment of taxes, the executor or trustee must come up with the cash. If insurance does not provide the cash or cash has not been made available in a money market fund, certificates, or other cash equivalents, the executor or trustee must sell noncash assets to raise the money. The IRS insists on cash—with one exception:

Certain issues of U.S. Treasury bonds are accepted in payment of estate taxes at their par (face) value regardless of their market value, which varies according to the general level of interest rates. Bond prices tend to rise when interest rates decline and vice versa. Thus, the U.S. Treasury bonds noted in Table 11A are special because they will be accepted at par for the payment of estate taxes. Due to their association with funerals, these special issues are known as **flower bonds**.

Your estate must own the flower bonds at the time of your death. If you anticipate a substantial estate tax bill, you could buy 50 flower bonds valued at par for something less than their $50,000 par value and include them among your assets. How much less than $50,000 you might pay depends on numerous factors, including the general level of interest rates. At tax bill time, your executor or trustee could present the bonds for payment of $50,000 of your estate's tax liability, even if the market value of the 50 bonds was only $40,000.

TABLE 11A—FLOWER BONDS

Series	Dated	Maturity
4¼	1987–92	August 15, 1962–August 15, 1992
4	1988–93	January 17, 1963–February 15, 1993
4⅛	1989–94	April 18, 1963–May 15, 1994
3	1995	February 15, 1955–February 15, 1995
3½	1998	October 3, 1960–November 15, 1998

Notes: Bonds are described by their interest rate, for instance 4¼ percent for the first series above, and the maturity date, August 15, 1992, for that series. In the first three series of bonds, individual bonds mature at different times, hence the rabge of years. The last bond of the series matures at the date under "Maturity." Bond's issue date, although noted, is unimportant.

The U.S. Treasury no longer issues flower bonds; they are only available on the secondary market through brokers. As the bonds now outstanding are presented for payment of estate taxes, they are retired. With no new issues and the supply of existing bonds declining, considerable demand may boost their prices above what bonds with similar interest rates would bring. One deterrent to purchasing these bonds is the loss of current income while you hold flower bonds that pay less than market rates. The box below illustrates how you can figure a breakeven point between a loss of income compared to the bonus you receive in paying estate taxes.

Conclusion

Settling an estate through probate involves seemingly unlimited numbers of details, large and small, plus delay after delay. Your executor will need to satisfy the IRS and possibly a state tax authority, manage your resources until they can be distributed, distribute assets, and file a report with the probate court to conclude the proceedings.

Managing your living trust can be much simpler, save considerable time for distribution of assets, and your trust, irrevocable at your death, can continue to function until estate tax returns are filed. When trust provisions are completed and assets distributed, it can be dissolved.

BREAKEVEN POINT WITH FLOWER BONDS

Breakeven equals the gain from using flower bonds compared to the number of years of lost income. For example, if a person owns flower bonds for many years prior to his or her death, he or she loses interest income from the low rates compared to what he or she could earn from other types of bonds paying more interest. It is thus desirable to own flower bonds for the shortest possible time prior to death. The breakeven point occurs when the loss of interest (from the low flower bond rates) exactly equals the difference in the cost of the bonds and their par value for paying estate taxes. The following example shows how this computation may be made.

Assume $10,000 par value of flower bond issue of January 17, 1963, bearing interest at 4 percent per annum.

Income = $400 ($10,000 x .04 interest)
Equivalent income from similar bonds
   (not flower bonds) = $800 ($10,000 x .08 interest)
Loss each year = $400
Price of bonds = $9,000 vs. par value of $10,000
Gain when paying estate taxes = $1,000
$$\frac{\$1,000}{\$400} = 2\tfrac{1}{2} \text{ years to breakeven}$$

Owning 4-percent flower bonds for 2½ years before owner's death would incur loss of $1,000 in interest and would exactly equal the gain from proffering bonds at par for payment of estate taxes.

Final Instructions

"If only I had known," is the common lament of surviving spouses. Deceased husbands or wives carry scads of information to the grave with them. These decedents do not withhold information deliberately. They just don't get around to putting data and information into usable form for the family and advisors.

Three types of information can be tremendously helpful to your survivor:

1. An organized list of things your executor, surviving spouse, or family member will need or can use will simplify his or her task of winding down your estate. Records, documents, and an almost unlimited stack of data sheets, certificates, and quick notes written on the backs of old envelopes may be hidden away in places as remote as a safe deposit box or papers simply tucked in a folder in the glove compartment of your car. These papers contain a wealth of informa- tion, but the information will be more useful if put into organized form.

2. A list of sources who can provide help for various needs, such as your legal advisor or even your handyman. You know who these people are, but unless you leave some written instructions, others might not.

3. An **informal letter** stating your wishes about funeral arrangements, burial or cremation, donations of body parts, and thoughtful suggestions for carrying on. If you make these decisions, your surviving spouse or others will not have to agonize over doing things the way they think you might have wanted them. Your final letter will usually contain information that is still important but that doesn't need to be included in a will or living trust.

Let's look at each of these three categories in detail.

Documents and Records

Modern life revolves around documents, certificates, written records, and paper trails of all kinds. Your organizing these written records can greatly simplify the actions of your executor. They might even help you get your own life's activities in order.

If you and your family keep documents such as insurance policies, Social Security cards, U.S. Savings Bonds, stock certificates, and so on in old shoe boxes, clasp envelopes, or cardboard boxes in a basement or attic, you need help. Organize your storage of important information into three depositories: **safe deposit box, home file, and wallet.** See Tables 12A, 12B, and 12C for guidelines on what items should be in each category.

Safe Deposit Box

Documents that cannot be replaced or that would be costly and/or time consuming to replace belong in a bank or private safe deposit box, one that not only protects these irreplaceable pieces of paper from theft but also from loss by fire or natural catastrophe. Among these valuable papers are:

1. Birth certificates, adoption papers, marriage certificate, and other records that satisfy legal requirements, a divorce record, if any, and death certificates of family members. Your executor may need some or all of these documents while sorting out survivor rights to various benefits and satisfying the IRS.

2. Military service records, such as discharge papers, medical files of treatment

---

TABLE 12A—Items to be Stored in Safe Deposit Box

Wills—Husband	Marriage certificate
—Wife	Birth certificate
Mortgage loan(s)	Divorce papers
House deed	Adoption papers
Cemetery lot	Death certificates
Home and capital cost records	Naturalization & entry papers
(cost basis data)	Passport
Vehicle titles or bills of sale	Military discharge
Installment contracts	Medical records
U.S. savings bonds	School records
Stock certificates	Inventory of personal property
Bonds	& home furnishings
Loan agreements or contracts	

INVENTORY OF PERSONAL PROPERTY—By Room*

Living Room

Item	Date Acquired	Purchase Price	Appraisal Value (Date)
_____	_____	_____	_____
_____	_____	_____	_____
_____	_____	_____	_____
_____	_____	_____	_____
_____	_____	_____	_____

(Additional worksheets as necessary to cover each room, basement, attic and garage.)
*A copy of this list should be kept in your safe deposit box.

JEWELRY

Item	Location	Date Acquired	Purchase Price	Appraised Value (Date)	Appraiser
_____	_____	_____	_____	_____	_____
_____	_____	_____	_____	_____	_____
_____	_____	_____	_____	_____	_____
_____	_____	_____	_____	_____	_____
_____	_____	_____	_____	_____	_____

ANTIQUES

Item	Location	Date Acquired	Purchase Price	Appraised Value (Date)	Appraiser

SECURITIES—Stocks

Company Name	No. of Shares	Date Acquired	Price/ Share	Total Cost	CUSIP No	Certificate No.

SECURITIES—Bonds

Company Name	No. of Bonds	Date Purchased	Total Cost	Maturity Date	Value	Call Date	Certificate No.

MUTUAL FUNDS

Fund Name	Date Purchased	Confirmation Filed	Share Price at Purchase

RETIREMENT BENEFITS

Who	Organization	Type	Date Begun	Agency	Contribu- tion/Cost	Approx. Value at 65
Husb.	Social Security	____	____	____	____	____
Wife	Social Security	____	____	____	____	____
Husb.	Keogh Plan	____	____	____	____	____
Husb.	IRA	____	____	____	____	____
Wife	IRA	____	____	____	____	____
Husb.	Tax Deferred Annuity	____	____	____	____	____
____	____	____	____	____	____	____
____	____	____	____	____	____	____

TABLE 12B—Home File

INSURANCE POLICIES

Company	Type*	Policy No.	Name of Insured	Name of Owner	Primary Bene- ficiary	2nd Bene- ficiary	Agent	Premium
____	____	____	____	____	____	____	____	____
____	____	____	____	____	____	____	____	____
____	____	____	____	____	____	____	____	____
____	____	____	____	____	____	____	____	____
____	____	____	____	____	____	____	____	____

*Life, health, accident, hospital, car, house

TABLE 12C—Wallet

Item	Number	Other Data
Driver's License		
Identification		
Health Card		
Auto Insurance		
Social Security Card		
Credit Card A		
" " B		
" " C		
Membership Cards		

received, and any other data relating to military service. While these records may be replaced, the process can involve months and require contacts with a number of remote sources. Your survivors may not have time to replace many documents needed to file claims or tax returns immediately.

3. Citizenship papers.

4. Passports.

5. Deeds to property owned separately or jointly, including abstracts or title insurance policies. If you own a burial plot, include that deed along with other title papers. In addition to the legal deed, include information on a burial plot in your home file or in your informal letter of final instructions.

6. Original, signed (executed) copies of your wills—both yours and your spouse's—or the original of your living trust. States with estate or inheritance tax laws still on the books may seal a safe deposit box when the owner or co-owner dies. A representative of the state or a bank officer empowered to act on the state's behalf along with the executor may inventory the contents of the safe deposit box within a few days. The executor can remove the will at that time. For convenient reference, keep an unsigned photocopy of your wills or living trust in your home file.

7. Mortgages, installment contracts, security agreements, and any other information regarding debts you may have paid within the past 10 years.

8. Notes or contracts evidencing what others owe you, either in money or goods. Your executor will need these written agreements to collect what is owed.

9. Titles to your automobiles, truck, trailer, boat, snowmobile, motorcycle or other vehicles will be needed if your executor sells or gives them away. Should any of the vehicles be stolen or destroyed your executor will need the titles as evidence of ownership in pressing claims.

10. Stock and bond certificates, unless your broker keeps these in his office or keeps a record of your ownership **"in street name."** When your broker keeps your stocks as data entries and provides you with a computer printout showing you as the beneficial owner, stocks are said to be "in street name." You should keep a list of certificate numbers and other data in your home file. Stock and bond certificates can be replaced, but the process is costly in both time and money; a bond is required to protect the issuer against the possibility of original certificates being presented at a later date. Keep the confirmations of stocks, bonds and mutual fund shares purchased to substantiate cost basis data for tax purposes. This information will also be useful in valuing your estate or any gifts made prior to death.

11. Patents or copyrights.

12. An inventory of household goods and personal property can be invaluable in case of a loss by fire or theft. If you document all of your belongings using the worksheets in Chapter 2, file one copy in your safe deposit box to avoid losing it in a fire. If your personal property includes any rare or unusual items, such as original paintings, a stamp collection, antiques, valuable collections, or other irreplaceable goods, include photographs and/or appraisals with precise descriptions. Some people with access to a camcorder record visual and audio descriptions on video tape. The taped record is stored in a safe deposit box.

The worksheet in Table 12A will help you remember to include specific bits and pieces of information in your safe deposit box.

Home File

Your home file contains all of your working documents along with copies of many of the documents filed for safe keeping in your safe deposit box. A two- or four-drawer file cabinet simplifies the organization of records and working files. A fire-proof file cabinet can protect important information, but don't count on it as a substitute for filing irreplaceable papers in a safe deposit box.

Here are the items you should keep in your home file:

1. Insurance policies of all kinds—life, automobile, health, accident, homeowners or tenants, long-term care, and personal property covered by individual policies. Keep a list of the policy numbers, companies, agents, and other pertinent data. (See the worksheet in Table 12B.) The insurance policy you receive is likely to be a duplicate of the original held by the company. In the event of a fire or other loss, it can easily be replaced. Similarly, if your car is financed, the original policy will either be retained by the lender or the lien holder will be noted on your copy. A mortgage holder will be noted as the priority payee of your homeowner's or fire insurance policy. The copies in your home file provide easy reference.

2. Tax returns for federal and state income, real estate, and personal property. Ordinarily, the **statute of limitations** runs out in three years. If the IRS claims too little income was reported, records may be examined as far back as six years. No time limit applies to fraud.

3. Bank statements, deposit slips, check stubs, and canceled checks. Plan to keep these for a minimum of three years—six years if the canceled checks are used as evidence of tax deductions claimed on income tax returns and for paying income taxes. Actually, 10 years is a better term for keeping canceled checks because of the possibility of legal actions on contracts.

4. Receipts, receipted bills, sales slips, and annual statements of investment earnings. Keep these receipts for at least six years if they are involved in the reporting of income on tax returns. Some cross-filing may be desirable. If you keep documents to substantiate income tax returns with your copy of each year's return, make a note of the material that may affect other files. You may keep receipts as evidence of purchases in case you need to file warranty claims or return merchandise. Or, you may keep receipts stapled to warranty documents to keep everything together.

5. Stubs of Social Security checks. Keep the stubs separate from the card you carry with you. If you should lose your card, you can get your number off the stub to simplify asking for a replacement. If your monthly Social Security benefits are transferred to your individual checking accounts electronically, evidence of their receipt is noted on bank statements.

6. Unsigned copies of your wills or living trust.

7. File of warranties and guarantees along with a sales slip or date of purchase receipt and the seller for each item. Instructions for use or repair and a parts list may accompany the warranty documents. Keep a written record of repairs and the name of the servicing organization.

8. A copy of your inventory of household goods and personal property. A well-organized inventory segregates property according to the room where it is located. List each item and record a description sufficient for positive identification, such as a model and serial number, the date it was purchased, seller, and the price paid. Knowing the total value of your property will help in determining how much insurance should be carried against loss. Because of the possibility of this inventory being lost or destroyed by fire, keep a copy of it in your safe deposit box. A camcorder record of your belongings on video tape, possibly with an audio commentary, can supplement or replace the written inventory. File a copy of the video tape in your safe deposit box.

9. Employment records for you and your spouse. These data may be needed to claim retirement and other job benefits.

10. Income, income tax, Social Security benefits, and similar data should be kept in a file related to your financial controls. Include an annual net worth statement.

11. A list of financial and other advisors. (See the worksheet in Table 12D). Be sure you keep this list up to date.

12. A list of the items stored in your safe deposit box. Update this list regularly.

13. Bill paying and financial records you use every day or every week. Checking account activities can be the focal point of your home management center. Rather than record your banking activities in the **check register** at the back of your album checkbook, organize a three-ring notebook with lined accounting sheets for a check register. Checks you and your spouse write in different checkbooks can be consolidated in one register to simplify reconciling each month's bank statement. A check register maintained chronologically provides a record of withdrawals and deposits for reference. Include a place for unpaid bills and

for bills paid along with a date and check number. A well organized file of income and spending data pays off at income tax filing time.

Your Wallet

Your wallet, billfold, or purse contains the documents you and your spouse use every day. Important papers that belong in your wallet or purse include:

1. Driver's license.

2. Identification for yourself and an address and telephone number for the person who should be notified in case of an accident. Include alternative persons in case the first named person should be with you or unavailable.

3. Health insurance identification card that assures a hospital of your ability to pay for services. If you are diabetic, epileptic, or allergic, include information on drugs for emergency treatment, who to call if you are unconscious, and a list of drugs or materials you may be allergic to.

4. Auto insurance card that includes policy number, company name, and the name of your agent.

5. Social Security card.

6. Credit cards used regularly. Do not include every card you own because they may be lost or stolen.

7. Organizational membership cards if actually needed for admission to meetings or facilities. Keep organization cards issued for record purposes in a home file.

Getting started at what might appear to be the horrendous task of organizing your records can be your biggest barrier. Collecting the records may appear formidable. But your surviving spouse will have a much greater task of pulling facts and figures together from stacks of bills and receipts stuffed into a cardboard box if you don't help. Not only will you be doing your executor and/or surviving spouse a tremendous favor, but you will benefit from having an organized approach to your family's business.

Advisors and Resources

Probably the most valuable book in your possession is your telephone and address book. This is the handy volume near your home and/or office telephone that contains the names and numbers of persons and organizations you call on for help from time to time. You may know that Horace Dollarwatcher is your broker, but will anyone else know who to look for? Or you may talk frequently with Samuel Beancounter, your accountant, or Josh Litigator, your attorney. Old Mac has kept your cars running for years. But does anyone else know his full name or where he works?

Expand your telephone book into an organized listing of advisors and resources. The worksheet in Table 12D will help to remind you of the resources your surviving spouse or executor may need to consult.

The Final Letter

No one feels as alone as a surviving spouse, even after a long illness or time to "get prepared." A sudden fatal accident can be even more devastating. Much of the information in the preceding chapters aims to prepare your spouse for the critical time when he or she is alone. Much of the information is technical or cold fact. Despite the detailed compilations of facts in Tables

TABLE 12D—List of Advisors

Advisor	Name	Company/ Organization	Address	Telephone Number	Purpose
Attorney					General
"					Business
"					Will/Living Trust Consultant
Banker					
"					Taxes–Personal
Doctor					Husband
"					Wife
"					Children
Clergyman					
Employer					Husb. Contact
"					Wife's "
Stockbroker					
Financial Planner					
Life Ins. Agent					
Administrator					Group Insurance
Health Ins. Agent					
Car Ins. Agent					
VA Contact					
Car Mechanic					
Handyman					
Appraiser					
Health Ins. Agent					

12A through 12D, some things cannot be tabulated or listed. Plan to include one more item—an informal letter that pulls many loose ends together.

Here are a few hints about how to compose a final letter.

Your letter is personal, so write it in your own handwriting or type it yourself—strikeovers, mistakes, and all. Don't, under any circumstances, dictate it to a secretary to be typed up in formal style. Your letter should be intimate, written only for your spouse's eyes. Maintain a casual tone without any hints or overtones of morbidity, sentimentality, or handwringing. Put yourself in your spouse's place, if you can, to anticipate and answer his or her questions.

Address your first thoughts to funeral arrangements. Your spouse will be asked first for decisions and she or he might not be thinking clearly. Simply state the kind of a service you would prefer. If you have already selected a cemetery lot, note the location and whether it is paid for or not. Name the person to consult about interment. If you expect to be buried in a national cemetery, note your preference and define briefly the exact sequence to follow in advising the superintendent. If you have not selected a cemetery lot, you can state your preference to relieve your spouse from having to make a difficult decision. If you have decided on cremation rather than burial, make your decision known. If you have made arrangements to donate your body to a medical school or research facility, you will have contacted the appropriate institution; state the facility and the person to see about arrangements.

Other funeral arrangements can be planned too. If you prefer a specific funeral home to handle affairs, say so. Perhaps you have a special friend or pastor you would like to officiate in the service. You could even list individuals your spouse could contact about being pallbearers. If you like a specific singer, note the person or alternatives if the one person is not available. Arranging funeral details can be highly stressful for the family. If you have made many of the decisions, plans may proceed smoothly.

Writing funeral instructions in a personal letter rather than a will or living trust can be helpful in several ways. First, changing a will can be difficult and expensive, whereas you can rewrite a final letter as often as you want or need to. Second, a personal letter is immediately available. Third, your wishes expressed informally in a letter are preferable to the legal verbiage typical of wills. You can simply write out your ideas, privately and in your own words.

Include names of relatives who should be notified of your death. Your spouse will know of many of them, but he or she could easily overlook someone who would be offended if not notified.

Until your children graduate from college, if they do, and are out and on their own, you could include your ideas about their education. You might name a college for them to attend along with your reasons. If you want your son to attend your alma mater, you could name some friends or classmates who could put in a few good words in his behalf.

Financial affairs may trouble a spouse who has not been active in family financial dealings. You could include in your letter some of your ideas about disposing of assets, even your home. Will your surviving spouse want to continue living in the family homestead? Or will he or she move into a smaller house, condominium or retirement

A SAMPLE FINAL LETTER

Dear Emily,

   I have taken a few minutes from time to time to jot down some notes that might help you at this moment.

   First, no funeral. We have talked earlier about my interest in not contributing to the wasteful use of land for cemeteries. And I hate those graveside dramas, usually in the rain around here. Please arrange for my body to be cremated. Charlie, down at Charming Funeral Home can handle it. No body viewing or display, please. And no urn either. Ask Jimmy's friend, the one who flies the Cessna, to scatter my ashes over the mountains where we hiked so often—among the wildflowers. A short memorial session might be appropriate. Donald could sing a couple of songs—his choice. I always liked his barbershop quartet and he's good as a single too. I like that new pastor at the church—he could officiate. I think a reception in the church parlor with some finger food and coffee would lighten up things afterwards.

   I have left a copy of our living trust in the Estate Planning file—top drawer, near the front. Signed originals are in the safe deposit box. You are the surviving trustee, but ask Ben for help. He and John Edwards, our accountant, listed in the advisors file, will need to develop a federal estate tax return, as our gross estate will exceed the limit. As you know, practically all of our assets were transferred to the trust several years ago. Ben will help if you need to probate the "pour over" will to account for anything I might have left out. He can also explain about the tax-saving trust that leaves all of the income from my half of our property to you and then equally to Jimmy and Beth.

   I know I have held out against moving away from this big old house—too much of my life has been centered here. But it could be too much for you to take care of. As you know, it is free and clear and worth a bundle. If you decide to move to Arizona near your sister, be sure to utilize the $125,000 capital gain exemption to reduce income taxes. If you find a house or condo you like, pay cash for it—don't finance it. As for our mutual funds, the funds you picked are doing better than ours—so keep it up.

   There's a lot of stuff in closets and the basement. I'd like Jimmy to have my old computer. You certainly don't need two, and the new one is so much faster. It's not worth much on the second-hand market, so hang on to it. If Jimmy wants the old bayonet from the Korean rifle, he's welcome to it. Beth might like those two antique silver bowls that my mother left me. The Youth Center Thrift Shop can probably make a few bucks selling my old clothes. Our Rotary Club has helped support the Youth Center for years. Don't bother trying to get a tax deduction; it's not worth the trouble.

   By the way, be sure to drop Evelyn Jones a note. You have the address on our Christmas card list. I haven't seen her for years, but she was a good friend of my mother's.

   I guess that's it, honey— Carry on. I know you'll do fine.

                                        Love,
                                        John

community? Your thoughts can be helpful. You might advise a widow to pay off the mortgage on your house if you believe that is a valid financial move.

Your will may specify who is to receive the valuable gun collection you spent years assembling because it is likely to be quite valuable. But will your spouse know whom to give the souvenirs you picked up in Korea? Will your spouse know who should get a special ring, pieces of silver service, and other heirlooms you received from your parents? Valuable property should be specified in a will to avoid controversy. But smaller items can be noted in a final letter to avoid changing a will if you change your mind.

Any letter you write should come from the heart. Remember your objective—to ease your spouse's transition over a difficult period. See the box on page 163 for a sample of how a letter might be written.

GLOSSARY

actuarial value Value of something viewed statistically for risks related to life expectancy.

administrator Person appointed by a court to represent an estate when no will was provided or the will did not name an executor. May also be called a personal representative.

adult adoption Legal procedure for adopting adults for the purpose of changing their status in reference to state inheritance taxes.

affinity group An organization of like persons, such as accountants, that may offer a variety of services, including the opportunity to buy group life insurance.

alternate date A date six months after a decedent's death that may be used for evaluating assets in an estate.

amortization schedule Payment schedule of level amounts that include a partial payback of principal plus interest to pay off a loan over a specific period.

annual gift An amount, currently $10,000 at federal level, that may be given to a person without filing a gift tax return or paying a gift tax.

annuity Investment that pays a fixed amount for a specified number of years or for life.

annuity trust One form of charitable remainder trust that pays a fixed amount regularly according to the value of a gift at the time it is set up, age of donor, and interest rates.

appraiser An expert, usually licensed, who determines and sets a value for various assets, including real estate.

appreciated or **appreciating asset** An asset whose value has increased or continues to increase in value due to a variety of factors, including inflation.

assigning ownership Giving all ownership rights in an insurance policy to another person, mainly for the purpose of removing future death benefits from the decedent's gross estate.

beneficiary A person designated to receive income or assets in a will or living trust.

bequest Property left to a person or charity in a will.

boilerplate Slang for standard paragraphs or clauses in documents, including wills and trusts.

buy-sell agreement Agreement between partners or co-owners of a business that determines the conditions and price for a buyout by one or more of the owners at the death of one.

capitalization A method of valuing real estate or a business based on its earning capacity. A capitalization rate of 10 percent means the capital value of the asset is 10 times the annual income.

cash-value insurance Life insurance that contains a savings account along with coverage for the life of the insured. Saving feature may be structured various ways.

charitable remainder trust Gift made in trust to a recognized charity that includes income payable to the donor during that person's lifetime. At the death of the donor, the remaining value of the gift belongs to the charity.

codicil A written and properly witnessed legal change or amendment to a will.

commingling Mixing of separate property with community property until specific portions can no longer be identified.

common law Laws based on custom and usage plus the body of decisions and opinions handed down by courts. Distinguished from statute law that results from legislative action.

community property Assets and property acquired by the marriage community and owned equally by marriage partners in nine states, located mostly in the western United States.

community property agreement A simple document that legally transfers title of property owned by the marriage community to the surviving spouse.

contingency An action that depends on something else happening, as a contingent trustee functions only when the primary trustee declines to act or is not available.

conveyance The act of transferring ownership from one person to another or the document that effects the transfer.

correction deed A deed that conveys title to property within a living trust when one person dies.

cost basis   An asset's original cost, such as a house, plus any capital additions. Cost basis of stock is the price of the shares plus transaction costs.

co-trustee   A person who serves with another trustee in managing a living trust to provide advice, expertise, and judgment.

creator   Person who establishes a trust and provides the funding. Also called grantor, settlor or trustor.

curtesy   Legal rights of a surviving husband in the property of a dead wife if the couple had children capable of inheriting.

CUSIP   Security identification number, from Committee on Uniform Securities Identification Procedures organized by the American Bankers Association, carried on every stock, corporate bond, and municipal bond.

custodial care   Care for a person who cannot manage on his or her own. Includes bathing, feeding, and other activities but minimal medical attention. Normally offered by nursing homes.

custodian   Trustee of UGMA and UTMA trusts set up for minors.

death benefits   Amounts paid on insurance policies according to agreement plus accumulated dividends and interest earned on dividends.

disability   Medical condition where one is unable to work.

donee   Person who receives a gift.

donor   Person who gives a gift.

decedent   Deceased person.

domicile   One's fixed place of dwelling where one intends living permanently.

dower   That part of a husband's property that his widow inherits for her lifetime.

durable power of attorney   A power of attorney is a legal document that gives another person full legal authority to act on that person's behalf, including signing checks and similar means of handling money. A durable power of attorney continues to be in effect when the person giving the power is incapacitated or disabled.

escheat   Reversion of property to the state when no legal heirs claim property.

estate planning   Orderly arrangement of assets and a plan for conveying them to heirs and others in a manner calculated to minimize taxes, expenses, and delays.

executor   Person or institution named in a will to carry out its provisions and instructions. The female term is executrix.

exemption   Amount of assets on which taxes are forgiven.

fair market value   A price agreed to by a willing buyer and a willing seller in a free negotiation and taking location into account.

fiduciary   A person acting primarily for another's benefit that requires confidence, good faith, prudence, and fair dealing.

flower bonds   U.S. Treasury bonds that are accepted at par value in the payment of federal estate taxes.

grantor   The person who establishes or creates a trust. Also called creator, settlor, or trustor.

gross estate   Total dollar value of all one's property and belongings.

group life insurance   Term life insurance provided at group rates, usually by an employer. Rates are averaged for age of workforce and do not usually require a physical examination.

guardian   A person who is legally responsible for the care and upbringing of another person, usually a minor. A guardian is normally appointed by a court, possibly under the direction of a will, and is responsible to the court.

heir   A person legally entitled to receive another person's property through action of the law upon the person's death. Usually, an heir is anyone who receives property through a will or a trust.

holographic will   Handwritten will that need not be witnessed. Not accepted in all states. Must be witnessed in New York unless author of will is member of armed forces.

imputed interest   Rate of interest assigned by Internal Revenue Service to a less than market rate loan or a no interest rate loan. Lender must pay taxes on imputed interest even if no money is actually received from borrower, who may be a friend or family member.

incidents of ownership   Normally associated with insurance. Includes any control, such as being able to change a beneficiary, encumber a cash balance for loan collateral or cancel a policy.

informal letter   A letter in one's own handwriting (usually) to a surviving spouse with directions for handling funeral arrangements and other details following one's death.

inheritance tax   A tax levied in some states on inherited property. Tax rates typically depend on the relationship of the heir to the decedent.

interested person   Any person who may be affected by or interested in the provisions of a will.

inter vivos   Latin for among the living as in an inter vivos trust, one that is created while you are alive.

intestate, intestacy   Without a will; condition of an estate being settled without a will.

in street name   Stocks held by a broker with beneficial interest of owner documented as data entered in the firm's computer. Beneficial owner's name not shown on transfer agent's listing and no certificates issued.

irrevocable   When applied to a trust indicates it cannot be changed or cancelled.

joint tenancy   Owning property jointly, in some forms with the right of survivorship where the survivor owns the property.

JTWROS   Joint tenancy with right of survivorship.

kiddie tax   Slang for federal income tax on minors up to age 14.

legatee   A person to whom money or property is left in a will.

letters testamentary   Documents from a probate court authorizing an executor to gain access to data and information necessary in the settlement of an estate.

liability   A debt; something owed by somebody.

life interest   A benefit, such as income from a trust, that continues for the life of the person holding the interest.

living trust   A revocable written legal form into which a person transfers all of his or her assets and property along with instructions for the manager (trustee) for the distribution of assets following the grantor's death, at which point the trust becomes irrevocable.

majority The age at which a minor becomes an adult. Age of majority varies in different states and may also vary for different purposes, as the age for voting may be different from the age when a minor becomes the owner of a UGMA trust.

marginal estate tax rate Percentage tax rate applied to the next dollar of taxable assets after the exemption.

marital deduction A deduction equal to about half of an estate awarded to the surviving spouse upon the death of a marriage partner.

money market mutual fund A mutual fund that invests assets only in money market instruments, such as treasury bills, certificates of deposit, commercial paper, etc., and characterized by a constant net asset value, usually $1 per share.

net gift A gift awarded with any tax liabilities paid by the estate.

net worth Total assets minus total liabilities. Also, how much one owns less how much one owes.

oral will A will given orally to a person, usually in the presence of witnesses. Oral wills are not recognized or are recognized only within limits by a small number of states. Oral wills may be limited to instructions issued just before death on a battlefield in California and a limited number of other states.

partition Process of dividing property and giving separate title to property that was formerly jointly owned.

pay-on-death Informal trust arrangement, usually limited to bank accounts where the balance of an account becomes the sole property of a noted beneficiary.

personal property Nontitled property, such as clothes, appliances, guns, electronic equipment, etc.

personal representative Another name for a person who is charged with managing an estate; same as executor or administrator.

pickup tax An estate tax levied by some states equivalent to the federal exemption for state estate taxes. No additional taxes are paid, but a portion of the estate tax stays with the state.

pooled income trust Charitable remainder trust where cash or readily marketable securities are commingled with similar contributions from others and managed like a small mutual fund.

pour-over will A will designed to cover property that has not been transferred to a living trust. Assets are "poured over" into the trust for management.

prenuptial agreement A contract agreed to by a couple prior to marriage that defines separate property and such points of possible contention as who pays for groceries, who pays for housing, etc.

probate court A specialized court set up to handle the management of wills or estates of persons dying without a will and other functions, such as transferring title by persons who cannot sign their names.

probate estate Property and assets distributed under direction of the probate court. Property originally owned jointly or benefits that flow directly to beneficiaries are not part of the probate estate.

Q-TIP trust A specialized trust that controls the disposition of a terminal interest mainly for the benefit of children of a former marriage.

remainder interest Property usually left to a charity after the death of one or more beneficiaries that may have participated in a trust while living.

resources Typically a broader term than assets or property that applies to the estate of a decedent and could include services or other debts owed to the estate.

reversionary trust Also called "Clifford trust," take-back trust, or short-term trust. A trust that exists for 10 years plus a day as a vehicle for transferring income to children or handicapped persons. Later ownership of trust assets passes to someone else, but not the original grantor.

separate property Property owned only by one marriage partner that is kept segregated from the couple's community property.

settlement Payment of death benefits from life insurance to beneficiaries. Various options are available for receiving a settlement.

settlor Another term for the person who establishes and funds a trust. Also called grantor, creator, or trustor.

severing Partition or division of jointly owned property under the guidance of a court when joint owners cannot agree on a division.

spendthrift trust Trust established for a beneficiary whose money management skills are suspect to prevent the beneficiary from spending a legacy wantonly.

statute of limitations A code statute that limits the period in which a specific legal action may be taken.

stepped-up valuation An increase to a current valuation of appreciating assets in the process of settling a will or living trust. The stepped-up value of securities or real estate is used in figuring the gross estate. Later when a beneficiary sells the asset, the stepped-up value is the new cost basis for figuring capital gains, if any.

stock split Change in the number of shares that does not change their total capital value. A stock may split 2 for 1, which means one share becomes two, but the valuation of each share is halved.

succession A series of heirs in line to receive inheritances, usually defined by statute.

supervised procedure Formal probate court procedure where every part of the estate's dismantling, including appraisals, tax return filing, and title changes are supervised by the court.

support A loosely defined term that includes housing, food, clothing, and basic necessities of life for children. Support is a parental obligation.

taxable estate Gross estate less all debts, expenses (including attorney, accountant, and appraiser fees), executor fees, and probate court costs and taxes, if any.

tax deferred annuity Combination of life insurance with an investment that is shielded from income tax liability until it is withdrawn or flows into an estate.

tax-saving trust Testamentary or living trust component that segregates up to $600,000 of decedent's assets and places them in trust for children or other heirs.

tenancy in common Joint ownership without right of survival. Joint interest may be given or willed to an heir.

tenancy in the entirety Joint ownership limited to married couples that includes right of survival.

term life insurance Pure insurance coverage only with no savings component, typically issued for one year, five years, or other specific term after which no residual remains.

testament Rare, meaning a will, its usage now relegated to the term, "last will and testament."

testamentary Something that happens in or as a result of a will.

testate Having made a valid will. "Dying testate" means a person dies having left a valid will.

three-year pull-back Certain transfers of assets, such as an insurance policy into an irrevocable insurance trust, that are cancelled or "pulled back" into a decedent's estate if the transfer occurred within a three year period of death.

titled property Property with a title of ownership registered at some agency or government office. Real estate may be registered by deed at a county office; stocks are registered on the ownership list of a company; a car is registered by the state. Strict rules regulate the transfer of titled property.

transfer agent An agent, usually a bank, authorized to transfer title to stocks or bonds by the issuing corporation or governmental organization. Transfer agent maintains the official list of stockholders of a corporation.

Treasury bills Short term debt instruments issued by the U.S. Treasury. T-bills are discount securities; that is, they are sold for less than the face amount and redeemed at a specified time later for the full face amount. The difference between the discount price and the face amount is the interest earned.

trust A written and formal agreement that enables a person or institution to hold property and manage it for the benefit of identified beneficiaries in accordance with instructions in the trust agreement.

trust agreement Document setting out instructions for managing an estate left in a living trust, including who is to receive each portion of the trust assets.

trust estate Total value of property and assets transferred to the living trust by the trustor.

trustee Person or institution empowered to manage estate property according to the instructions contained in the trust agreement.

trustor Person who establishes and funds a trust. Also grantor, creator, or settlor.

Uniform Gifts to Minors Act (UGMA) A simplified trust agreement that permits a custodian (trustee) to hold and manage assets for the benefit of minors. UGMA trusts are irrevocable and in force in all 50 states. When minors attain their majority, all assets become theirs.

Uniform Probate Code An effort by the American Bar Association to simplify and unify the probate codes of the various states to reduce the costs and delays of probate. The UPC has been accepted, usually in modified form, by only about 17 states.

Uniform Simultaneous Death Act An attempt to simplify and unify the handling of the affairs of a couple that die, usually accidentally, in a manner that does not permit identification of which spouse died first. A valid will supersedes the USDA, and not all states have adopted it.

Uniform Transfers to Minors Act (UTMA) Similar to UGMA but permits the ownership of real estate and other property not acceptable under UGMA. UTMA trusts are operable in half of the states and are irrevocable. Minors receive unrestricted use of assets at majority.

unitrust Form of charitable remainder trust whereby donor receives at least a minimum annual return based on an annual valuation of assets.

will Basic document for transferring property to successors through probate court.

witness Person who sees a person sign a will and attests the oversight by signing. Later, in proving the legitimacy of a will, witnesses may be called to testify to their signing in probate court, or an affidavit may be sufficient.

INDEX